To:

Russ Ouellette

Enjoy your thoughts on coaching & culture

Brian A Jrohs

Professional Endorsements for
Creating a Culture of Success

"This book will help transform your workplace...I have personally benefited my organization for many years through the acceptance and application of the philosophies and techniques presented within the text of this blueprint for a successful work environment. Dr. Charles Dygert is my coach and mentor. I thank him for helping shape my management style in such a way that I too have become a truly effective coach and leader."

—Charles Hossom, Vice President and General Manager
Dayton Rogers of Ohio, Inc.

"If you are interested in building a high powered, engaged organization, *Creating a Culture of Success* will light the way in a convenient and straightforward manner."

—Daniel Toussant, Director of Human Resources
Rea Associates, Inc.

"*Creating a Culture of Success* is a practical, no-nonsense approach to common sense leadership."

—Jackie Hammonds, Retired
Honda of America Manufacturing, Inc.

"Thoughtful advice from two experienced practitioners."

—Dr. Raymond Forbes, Professor
Graduate School, Franklin University

"A great book for the whole management team."

—James F. Hopkins, President/CEO
Hopkins Printing

"This book helped me clarify and codify my own beliefs about culture change and its effect on people."

—Paul Greenland, President
Aetna Building Maintenance

"The book that influenced us the most in building our business was *Culture of Success* by Charles B. Dygert, Ph. D. and Richard A. Jacobs, P.E."

—Joseph Dager, President and
Michael Dager, Vice President
Velvet Ice Cream Company

SECOND EDITION

CREATING A CULTURE OF SUCCESS

Fine-Tuning the Heart and Soul of Your Organization

Charles B. Dygert, Ph. D.
Richard A. Jacobs, P.E.

MOO PRESS
BUSINESS BOOKS

CREATING A CULTURE OF SUCCESS
Fine-Tuning the Heart and Soul of Your Organization

QUANTITY PURCHASES
Companies, professional groups, nonprofits, and other organizations may qualify for special discounts when ordering quantities of this title. For information, write Special Sales, Moo Press, PO Box 54 Warwick, NY 10990, call 845-987-7750 or email to SpecialSales@moopress.com.

Publisher's Cataloging-in-Publication Data
Dygert, Charles B.
    Creating a culture of success : fine-tuning the heart and soul of your organization / Charles B. Dygert, Richard A. Jacobs. — 2nd ed. — Warwick, N.Y. : Moo Press, 2004.
    p. ; cm.
First ed. published: Columbus, OH : Motivational Enterprises, Inc., 1996.
Includes bibliographical references.
    ISBN: 0-9724853-4-1
1. Organizational behavior. 2. Success. 3. Management. 4. Corporate culture.
5. Organizational change. 6. Success in business. I. Jacobs, Richard A. II. Title.
III. Fine-tuning the heart and soul of your organization.
    HD58.7 .D94 2004   2003111729   658—dc22 0407

Jacket cover design by Desktop Miracles, Inc. Stowe, VT.
Jacket photo credits: Photo of Charles Dygert by Lary Lee Photography.
Photo of Richard Jacobs by Richard Pound, Don Pound Studio.

Printed in the United States of America.

10 9 8 7 6 5 4 3 2 1

DEDICATIONS

This book is dedicated to my leadership models: my father "Captain" Ed Dygert, and my uncle Ken Dygert.

— Charles B. Dygert, Ph.D.

This book is dedicated to my mentors, who believed in me: my father Dick Jacobs and Lew Gayner.

— Richard A. Jacobs, P.E.

TABLE OF CONTENTS

BOOK-AT-A-GLANCE

1 Culture Drives Success
Introduces concept of work culture in organizations as a critical and often overlooked ingredient for success.

2 From Watchdog to Coach
Explains how developing a "shared vision" based on trust and communication in a team environment improves work culture.

3 Potholes to Avoid
Discusses need for people to be involved in the decisions that affect them.

4 Barriers to Change
Lists common barriers to change and the impact those barriers might have on transitioning to a culture of success.

5 Wake-Up Call
Reviews warning signs of culture problems and how to turn the tide.

6 People Want to Care
Discusses impact employee-employer care has on the success of a culture change.

7 Eliminating the Enemy Within
Describes negative side effects of internal competition and provides steps to move to a culture of internal cooperation.

8 The Zone of Improvement
Explains benefit ("what's in it for me") of moving to a culture of success.

9 Six Steps to Success
Provides six-step plan for getting started on your path to creating a culture of success.

AUTHORS' NOTE

Nearly a decade later, we revisit our *Culture of Success* text with hopes of getting this important message and guidebook into more hands at more levels of the organizations that still cry out for better internal culture.[1] Having worked in this area for more decades than we care to admit (twenty+ years), we have seen the great success companies and nonprofits can enjoy with the right internal culture. It saddens us greatly to see so many organizations ignore or just not be aware of the critical role culture plays in the success or failure of everything they try to accomplish.

This book began as a collection of lecture notes used at client sites, for presentations, and in university classes that we taught. We have used the first edition as a guidebook for many organizations (small, medium, and large) and as a "leave behind" tool to help leaders implement a culture change.

For this revised and updated second edition, we have changed the title slightly to bring more attention to the importance of culture in any organization. In many ways, culture is the heart and soul of an organization. Without the right culture, the organization slows down, loses its vitality, and could go into a type of cardiac arrest.

Our goal for this revised edition is to help you fine-tune the heart and soul of your organization, so that you too can achieve the success you have worked for, the success that you have dreamed of achieving.

We hope that this book will be your guide to bringing greater awareness to the impact culture has on your organization. Once aware, use this book as your guide on how to begin and maintain the culture changes.

Do not feel that you must begin on page one and read each chapter verbatim and in order. We have many war stories throughout the book, and aside from the last chapter which contains the

Six Steps to Success program, you should feel free to skip around and read the text in any order.

Appendix A contains background material on organizational theories and the history of this area, in case you are not familiar with the work of leaders in this field such as Deming, Juran, and Crosby.

Appendix B contains a recent study from the Denison Organizational Culture Survey which illustrates the positive financial impact of a high performance culture (direct evidence of the cause and effect relationship between a work culture and profitability expectations).

Since each chapter was designed to stand on its own, some repetition of concepts is inevitable. For that, we apologize. It is not recommended to read only the last chapter. The last chapter contains a six-step approach to implementing a culture change, but assumes that you have a good grasp of the culture concepts presented in earlier chapters.

Wherever possible in the text, we have tried to use the generic terms "organization" and "worker" instead of company/ association or employee/volunteer. It is our sincere hope that this book helps nonprofit as well as for-profit organizations experience the culture of success.

We welcome your feedback, questions, and comments. You can use the form at the end of this book, or email us at Culture@moopress.com.

As you may be aware, many tools exist to assist you in implementing a culture change. The concepts and tools presented in this book are not meant to be conclusive, but rather a starting point. That is truly our goal in writing this book, to get more organizations started on the path to *Creating a Culture of Success!*

Respectfully submitted,

~Dr. Charles Dygert and Richard Jacobs, P. E.

INTRODUCTION

What you are about to read is not a book, but an urgent message. Some will ignore its advice and continue to plod down a well-worn path that leads to mediocrity and disappointment. To others, however, this volume will be the turning-point that transforms their leadership and revolutionizes the organizational climate in which they work.

The shelves of bookstores are brimming with how-to manuals on everything from achievement strategies to zero-based budgeting, but virtually no attention is given to the organization's *culture*—the key ingredient to change, improvement, quality, and satisfaction.

To most people the term culture simply means, "The way we do things around here." Any shift in the status quo is seen as a threat, not an opportunity. Few understand that it is the success of the *culture* that drives the success of the enterprise.

On these pages we will examine how the internal environment of a school, a business, or any organization, can predict achievement or failure. You will understand why a culture change must involve the entire organization—whether its offices, plants, and people are across the hall or around the globe.

In some cases it may begin by developing a quality culture for only a part of the organization. Then, as the culture "comes into its own" and drives success in that area, the new culture can be brought to other areas of the organization.

If you've read William Byham's and Jeff Cox's book *Zapp* you know what happened when one department "saw the light" and eventually had an impact on the entire company.[1] It can all start with one dedicated, focused person who is not afraid of change.

The Crisis of Change

Without question, during the past decade there have been broad, sweeping changes in productivity, quality, training techniques, and management in the American workplace. These changes were dictated by the realization that education, business, and industry were not keeping pace with international advances in product quality and "team" cooperative processes. Even the federal government admitted that if change did not occur soon our country would not remain a world leader.

In thousands of organizations, traditional, autocratic management styles are being replaced with supervisory and management techniques that emphasize coaching or mentoring. The result stimulates human self-value, personal development, and feelings of being capable (confidence)—thereby developing an employee's sense of ownership in his/her company or organization.

This management transformation is the process by which Dr. W. Edwards Deming (the fabled "hero" of quality and team processes in Japan and the United States) suggests will drive out fear and the lack of trust between management and the work force. The "we" versus "them" mentality continues to permeate far too many organizations.

While serious and well-meaning "quality" efforts are being attempted, real progress is often hindered by halfhearted efforts—believing that the process is a quick fix. This can lead to heartache and suspicion. Staff members question, "Can it really happen here?"

Fine-Tuning the Heart and Soul

The introduction of innovative programs tend to raise expectations to new levels of enthusiasm, but before a real change is made, management is often off to the next initiative, leaving behind a doubtful work force. Too often our efforts at follow-through become victims of a "budget-cutting exercise" or just "poor management." In these situations, more harm is done than if it had just been left alone.

The implementation of a culture of success is not for the faint of heart. It requires a total commitment that goes far beyond a simple statement of intent or the periodic measurement of performance results.

On the pages that follow you will learn:

- How to eliminate mistrust among the various layers of an organization.
- How to replace destructive internal competition with cooperation.
- The cause and cure of a win-lose situation.
- Skills for leading the transformation to a culture of success.
- How to build an environment where growth, learning, and progress become primary goals.

Any individual, organization, or company needing to compete in the twenty-first century must consider investing serious energies in developing a team based quality culture, what we call a culture of success.

The decision is not, "Is it necessary?" but rather how to efficiently move in this direction and establish a never-ending passion to get "quality" and "team procedures" in place, and to maintain the effectiveness of the process. We believe this book will make that transition much easier.

Welcome to the culture of success!

1 CULTURE DRIVES SUCCESS

Three forces drive performance and impact results: culture, leadership, and power. This book focuses on the first force: culture. Studied for centuries by anthropologists and archaeologists, culture involves rituals, symbols, and stories associated with a group of people. Culture offers a glimpse into people's beliefs and values—what's important to them and why. Beliefs and values are shaped by tradition, environment, and individual personalities. Culture, which drives behavior, amounts to the "clubhouse rules" or "the way we do things around here."

Typically, people who have been in an organization for a long time seek to preserve traditions while new employees seek to change the status quo. A culture of success endeavors to improve the old ways without losing the spirit of their traditions. How can a leader implement this healthy balance?

First, organizations must have a high level of *trust* among their members, and second, individuals within it need to have demonstrated personal *integrity*. Together, these form the foundation for a *shared fate*. Only when individuals in an organization embrace the principle of shared fate can they be on their way to a culture of success.

> **Shared Fate:**
> **We win or lose,**
> **together.**

Culture Shock

Unique societies exist inside every office building, manufacturing plant, and educational institution. For better or worse, each organization has its own working environment—complete with distinctive customs, rules, and regulations. Just as people often experience anxiety when moving to a new country, the same can be true when changing jobs. This anxiety is often due to what is called "culture shock." A recent client of ours experienced culture shock when he left Home Depot for a position at Microsoft. Although both are prominent Fortune 500 companies, their internal cultures are very different, and it took some time for him to learn and adjust to the new culture.

Unless you change jobs, you may be completely unaware of the impact culture has on your organization. Or, perhaps you are painfully aware of the negative effects of a culture in need of change. Regardless, one thing is certain. It will take time to learn and adjust to the culture. The sooner the organization begins that journey, the sooner you and the organization will find your road to success.

Another New Mandate?

Imagine transforming the heart and soul of your organization into one where quality is not simply a desired goal, but a lifestyle. The secret is getting employees involved. Studies as far back as 1992 have found that many improvement programs deliver shoddy results due to "marginal employee involvement levels." [1]

> Management often finds it easier to mandate new policies than take the time to examine and improve (or build an appropriate) the underlying culture.

Despite the lip service that people are our best assets, companies continue to ignore their employees. Instead, they search for the silver bullet, the quick fix, or management tool-of-the-month. Why? Because mandating new policies is easier than taking time out to examine and improve the underlying culture.

If you want performance and results to flourish, if you want the competitive edge, it's time to explore your company's culture. Otherwise, quality and performance initiatives will merely irritate already beleaguered employees and become a bother to managers. Employees unable to internalize improvement processes being pushed on them, tend to perceive the orders for change as yet another scheme of assessment used to rank and rate everyone.

What's the Missing Link?

The missing link is having a clear understanding of the critical role that culture plays in the success of an organization. The culture of an organization is like the climate: it is present everywhere, yet mostly unnoticed until bad weather gets everyone's attention. The lack of a solid working culture inhibits real progress toward quality performance and results. If culture is not supporting the entire system, then an improvement program's technical and strategic segments are often rendered ineffective.

What fuels the culture of an organization? The management system (leadership). What influences the behaviors of those being led? The culture or organizational personality that management has activated, changed, altered, and challenged, based on its reactions to the existing cultural personality.

Ingredients for a Culture of Success:
- Trust each other
- Have personal integrity
- Agree on a shared fate

That brings us to a catch-22: If management exhibits no change in behavior or policies, the rank and file aren't going to initiate any change, either. Instead, management and nonmanagement will proceed to blame one another for any perceived problem.

If, however, both management and subordinates are involved in forming strategies on how to accomplish an improved culture (where trust and mutual interest thrive), the organization can begin to evolve in a positive way. *We* can solve problems together.

How Culture Impacts You

Sometimes, an illustration makes it easier to think about an old problem in a new way. In Figure 1.1 on page 18, Dr. Johnson Edosomwan illustrates the interplay between the management system and the employees' reactions.[2] In this diagram, generally known as the Edosomwan Model, four circles representing key systems in an organization (management, social, technical, and behavioral) revolve around a fifth circle of desired organizational changes.

Figure 1.1
Organizational and Process Transformation ("Edosomwan") Model

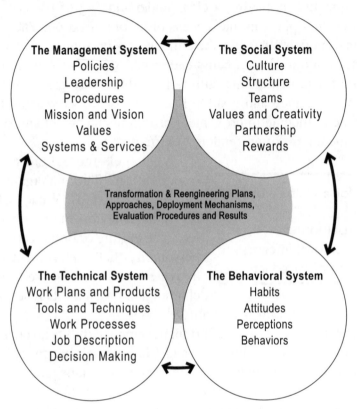

The lesson he drives home with this illustration is that all four systems—management, social, technical, and behavioral—are interlocked and mutually responsive to one another. Together, they hold the key to the evolution of the organization. Whatever transformation, right-sizing, process, or other improvements you wish to introduce in an organization, the success and effectiveness of that effort will be dependent on how the systems interact (the impact of the culture).

Of the four systems, note that the "management system" has the most power and impact on the other three systems. Culture and the change that management wants to effect are marked by a cause and effect relationship. Therefore, the vigilance of management in monitoring and interpreting the organization's behavioral trend, is essential in creating and maintaining a positive and productive organizational culture.

Just Another Scheme?

Demanding "higher standards" and "cooperation" to achieve quality products and services (or to increase productivity or profits) works temporarily if at all. A management demand spotlights a system characterized by the phrase, "Either I win or you lose!" This inspires workers to try to meet the expectations of an administrator or a supervisor – not to achieve excellent quality and productivity. Workers in such a system view themselves as doing the task for the boss, not the customer. Demands fuel internal competition which in turn spurs workers to do only enough to look better than the next person – in other words, just enough to get the supervisor off their backs.

Management *drives* culture.

Culture *drives* behavior.

Most of us would prefer a workforce that really cares about the success of the organization, and employees who take pride and ownership in the product or service they produce. When management attempts to introduce change, workers wonder, "Are they truly concerned about their workers, or is it merely a facade? Is a reward system in place to back up their promises? What is in it for me?"

A Way of Life

A culture of success is more than a technique for management to apply, more than a "program of the month" that employees can ignore and management can forget after a while. It's neither a simple tool nor a quick fix; it's a *way of life*. Employees in an internally competitive organization typically don't care whether their enterprise survives, and it shows. It's a sort of "get even" behavior that pits labor and management against one other.

The "we versus they" mentality fostered by traditional work environments needs to be turned inside out. The "we" should be your organization, and the "they" must become the competition. The good news is that it's easy to measure how much employees care. That's reflected by the amount of unprodded energy they put into their task.

It's Not New

More than two thousand years ago a Chinese warrior-philosopher by the name of Sun Tzu made essentially the same observation. In his classic book, *The Art of War,* Tzu stated:

> This is a matter of emptiness and fullness. When there are rifts between superiors and subordinates, when generals and officers are disaffected with each other and dissatisfaction has built up in the minds of the troops, this is called emptiness.

> When the civilian leadership is intelligent and the military leadership is good, when superiors and subordinates are of like mind, and will and energy operate together, this is called fullness.

> ...The skilled can fill their people with energy to confront the emptiness of others, while the incompetent drain their people of energy in face of the fullness of others.[3]

As leaders and workers in organizations, we must strive for "fullness." It is "like-mindedness" that produces certain victory. And, the sharing of a common goal—a shared fate—that builds a culture of success.

The Bag of Energy

Each morning we rise with a given quantity of strength and enthusiasm. Let's think of it as a bag of energy. As we prepare for the day's activities and travel to our workplace, we expend a certain amount of energy from our "bag." At our job, if we encounter anxiety or a negative attitude, that can drain so much energy that before mid-afternoon, we're empty and exhausted.

What, then, is left in our energy bag for our family and leisure activities? What happens to our quality of life? To gain maximum productivity in the workplace and beyond, we need leaders who ensure a positive environment. They help us conserve this energy. So once again, we reflect that the key to high output and positive employee morale rests with organizational culture and the management style.

Managers, fortunately, are waking up to the fact that workers are not robots in need of programming, but people with hearts, souls, and minds. Workers have feelings and emotions, and organizations that fail to acknowledge and address this are not treating employees as the full human beings they are. As authors Noel Tichy and Stratford Sherman note:

> Healthy people can't just drop their feelings off at home like a set of golf clubs. We are just beginning the search for ways to harness the vast power of workers' emotional energy.[4]

Beyond the Power Struggle

The value of working toward a system of total cooperation in the workplace has long been recognized, but only recently has it received the attention it deserves. What has prompted companies to sit up and take notice? Most organizations cite the increased global competition and recent economic challenges.

The biggest challenge in cooperative systems (introduced nearly seventy years ago by Christopher I. Barnard in *The Functions of the Executive*) is indoctrinating rank and file employees with a general sense of purpose, and granting them the ability to make major decisions.[5] Otherwise, how cohesive will the more detailed decisions be? Furthermore, if you allow executives to make decisions in isolation from workers, the organization runs the risk of losing touch with the essence of business, the customers and service or product produced. Misunderstandings and failure often result from not including front line employees in the decision process.

This challenge remains true today: If we don't work together, we're headed for failure. And to work together, we need to bring together four vital elements—often seen as opposing forces in an organization—into partnership. We call them the four "C's":

Change is one of those elements of life that you can always count on happening. In an organization, people struggle with change and each other because of change.

Competition, internal or external, impacts how people interact and how powerful (or not) those people are in a given situation.

Cooperation (often seen as the flip side of competition) can be an internal or external force that follows an individual's agenda or a team/company agenda. Cooperation can be a powerful force for good in an organization, as well as in the marketplace.

Control, and how control is granted, can be the power that makes or breaks an organization. Some situations call for more autocratic ("in charge") management methods and some require more democratic ("empowering") management methods. Autocratic leadership, where the person in authority tells everyone else what to do and how to do it, often results in people learning not to think for themselves and waiting until they are told what to do. This could lead to serious consequences for an organization as well as the individuals involved.

The traditional hierarchical management culture fuels the conflict among opposing forces:

Entity	Agenda	Opposing Forces
Organization	Survival	Market competition
Owner	Wealth	Sharing with employees
Manager	Control	Empowering others

- The organization is trying to survive with strong competitors in the marketplace and trying to gain market share.

- The owner (stockholder) wants to keep as much wealth as possible from the company while the employees demand higher pay.

- And caught in the middle, we have managers trying to retain "control" while workers desire greater empowerment.

Recipe for Success

If this list reflects the realities of your organization, don't be discouraged. Being honest about where power resides is a first step toward forging a road map for new partnership. In traditional structures, authority emanates from a position, not a person. When power is misused in such a system, mistrust and fear arise. The fear is not just felt by employees; executives may experience fears of losing power, status, or compensation.

To move toward a new environment of achievement, both sides need to conclude that to get something, they have to give something. That "something" must be based on trust, personal integrity, and a shared fate. These are essential ingredients for creating a culture of success.

Who must take the first step? Leadership. Even with little assurance that employees will follow, leaders must persuade all sides to sit down together and "get used to each other." Leaders must lead the way if they are going to develop a culture of success.

Together they must:

- Become comfortable with new ideas.
- Develop a strategy.
- Cooperate on implementing a plan.
- Test and evaluate results.

That's the path that leads to a culture of success.

Key Concepts

1. Three forces drive performance and results: culture, leadership, and power.
2. Culture drives behavior, but it is management that must drive the culture.
3. Trust and integrity form the foundation of shared fate, which individuals must embrace to achieve a culture of success.
4. Employees are the missing link in most improvement programs.
5. Management often falls into a trap of mandating new policies and programs instead of taking the time to examine the underlying culture.
6. A win/lose culture (internally competitive workplace) motivates employees to do just enough to keep the supervisor off their backs.
7. Management, social, technical, and behavioral systems in an organization are interlocked and mutually responsive to each other. But, the management system has the most power over the other systems.
8. Having a common goal—a shared fate—unites people and helps you build a culture of success.
9. Management is responsible for creating and maintaining a positive work environment.
10. Organizations that fail to treat employees as human beings with hearts, souls, and minds will find performance and results deteriorate as the culture deteriorates.

Things To Do Now

1. Top level management must meet and make the commitment to examine the culture in their organization.

2. Next, all levels of management should gather together to discuss the concepts behind a culture of success and get feedback from lower and middle management on how best to involve the employees.

3. Open the channels of communication throughout the organization by having management and employees discuss the culture concepts.

4. A shared fate must be agreed upon. Begin the conversation to determine what that shared fate (common goal) will be.

5. If there's a "we versus they" internal competition mentality, convert it to "our company versus the market competition" approach (a shared vision).

6. Management should identify concrete ways to ensure a positive work environment. How can policies and procedures be changed to treat employees more as human beings and less like machines?

7. Ensure that workers make some major decisions and have a clear sense of purpose.

8. Ask employees for ideas on how to improve the culture and quality of products/services.

2 FROM WATCHDOG TO COACH

What is a *culture of success*? Simply stated, a culture of success is an environment of cooperation where everyone is intrinsically concerned about the success of others. Another's success is a cause for feelings of personal accomplishment.

The objective we are discussing is not a secret, mysterious process. Organizations that have profited from the procedures, policies, and implementation strategies outlined in this book have honed the process to a science.

The foremost trait of a culture of success is communication based on trust. Unless subordinates can trust their leader's commitment to the organization's vision and values, and unless the leader can trust subordinates to be candid, the organization is poised to self-destruct.

The process begins with developing a vision to which everyone has input—who we are and what it takes to survive and be profitable. From this shared vision, leaders can establish strategies of training and organizational reform, and develop a new sense of purpose as to why the organization exists. Most likely, the organization exists to:

- Be profitable or perform a nonprofit service.
- Offer a competitive product for customers.
- Supply a competitive dividend to shareholders or stay within nonprofit budgets.
- Provide a growth environment to associates.
- Offer security to shareholders/members, customers, suppliers, associates, and their families.

Visions are "right brain" thinking; they stem from our creative genius and from our hearts. They involve basic human emotions. The mission statement, goals, and specific plans involve our "left brain," characterized by logic and analysis.

Culture Tip:

Listen more than talk.

"Where there is no vision, the people perish."[1] In your organization, who has the vision? The leader. Yet, for that vision to be realized, it must be shared by everyone in the organization. In a quality culture, the vision becomes such a strong reality for employees, that they adopt it as part of their lifestyle. That can happen only if employees are comfortable with the new vision, and have helped build that vision. After the concept is clear, it's time to write a mission statement and establish specific goals.

Cooperation Becomes Second Nature

For a true cultural change to transpire, the "new culture" must become as much a way of life as the old one was. How do you know when that day has arrived? When cooperation becomes second nature, not just the preferred method, but the *natural* way of doing things.

When good things are happening, you will see:

1. Employees are less concerned with how many hours they are working.

2. Concern subsides about who is getting ahead and who is paid what.

3. Issues such as the size of one's office and how far one's parking space is from the door become irrelevant.

4. The "win-win" of how to obtain the resources needed to produce quality products on time replaces the "win-lose" thinking of who is being awarded what resources.

5. Slowly, over time, loyalty (which is vital for a true quality culture) grows.

6. Management moves from being the "watchdog" to being the "coach."

Teamwork Replaces Competition

The transformation from a traditional management culture to a culture of success management system is a transition from an environment of internal competition to one of internal cooperation.

The words "team" and "teamwork" may sound the same, but each has a special meaning in the culture of success.

The New England Patriots may have been a team, but it was teamwork that allowed them to win the Super Bowl.

A "team" becomes a prominent part of the organizational structure when people from different departments or functions are cast together for a common purpose. The word "team" becomes emblematic of something changing.

"Teamwork," however, implies something even greater. It is not simply an assembly of people, but a group that displays a spirit of unity and accord. A team made up of brilliant athletes, each trying to outshine the other, each trying to hog the glory, is destined to become a team of brilliant losers.

The essence of teamwork is cooperation, and you cannot cooperate with the person against whom you're competing.

Here's an article that spotlights how a football team that converted to a true-team mind frame, produced astounding results.

Patriots spell success "T-E-A-M"

The New England Patriots refused to be introduced individually as they took the field for the Super Bowl. Instead, they entered the Louisiana Superdome as a team.

Few had ever seen anything like what the 14-point underdog Patriots did Sunday night. New England pulled off one of the greatest upsets in Super Bowl history—and avenged two previous Super Bowl blowout losses in the process—by shocking the team with the best record in football, the St. Louis Rams, 20-17.

"A lot of people didn't believe in these players, but it didn't matter what anybody said. They believed in themselves," New England coach Bill Belichick said.[2]

A Lesson in Workplace Harmony

How effective is workplace harmony? Let's answer that with another question. What happens when the water in a brook flows into a rock? The rock forms a barrier that causes the water to change its course.

Likewise, people in managerial positions often become impediments to the workflow. They do this by looking for something wrong; interrupting the work by asking unrelated questions just to establish authority.

Recently, while managing a distribution and fabrication plant, we observed first hand the benefits of true workplace harmony. Since it was the plant's busy season, there was a generous amount of meaningful work for everyone to do, every day. This eliminated the need for workers to pretend they were busy, create make-work, or prolong projects. The flip side of that, we learned, was not to exert too much pressure or incur excessive overtime costs. Delivery dates had to be realistic and met. Busy season was a time to focus almost singularly on outstanding customer service.

Two hourly workers functioning in a crew-leader capacity directed the day-to-day activities. Work flowed as smoothly as an orchestra playing a concerto—in perfect harmony. We wondered, why?

Well, first, the crew leaders knew exactly what they were doing, what they wanted to accomplish, the skills of the individual co-workers, and how much time they had to work with. They realized the importance of being fair, and concentrated totally on the mission at hand without fear of a person in management coming along and disrupting matters. They could count on a full backing of their decisions and actions. Therefore, their authority, however delicate, was never questioned by people above or below.

The fact that people liked their work was evident, but more impressive was that they liked working together. They saw the results of their efforts each day and were provided with customer feedback. Since there was plenty of work, the hours flew by, and people were able to maintain a high energy level despite working long hours.

This provided us with an interesting insight: it is not work that tires people out; it is frustration. And frustration is generally introduced by the boss, the system, the policies, or the work environment. The key to eliminating frustration is to focus the work group on one agenda.

1. Each individual has to be willing to check his or her personal agenda at the door every day.

2. Each person needs to know exactly what the agenda is for the day.

3. Each person is encouraged to participate in deciding how the work will be divided and accomplished.

4. Complimentary words between workers and leaders throughout the day help immensely.

Chemistry develops when people begin to enjoy doing things together and accomplishing things in teams or groups. That's when a camaraderie starts to develop, inclusive or exclusive of those in a supervisory position.

In this plant, everyone "on-site" but no one "off-site" partook of the camaraderie. There was a bit of a siege mentality, an us-versus-them notion that stemmed from seven years of being unsure whether the plant would be shut down or not. The culture at the plant differed from that in the rest of the company. In the plant, the focus was on pleasing the customer. In the rest of the company, the culture was to please the boss.

The two crew leaders were poetry in motion. Without bias or hidden agendas, they discussed and assigned the daily work, then went to work themselves, either on an individual assignment or working with the crew. They handled incoming customer calls in stride, and only did truly necessary paperwork.

They had no need to create work, pretend to be busy, or falsely exert authority. They played no mind games. The *gamesmanship*, we observed, had been totally replaced by *workmanship*. As for the quality, nothing left the plant that was not of the highest quality, a quality on which the crew leader would have insisted had he been working alone.

What were the key factors to this plant's success, strategies that any manager could implement?

- Remove impediments (typically the people who hinder the effort—often the management).
- Supply sufficient meaningful work.
- Select crew leaders who are skilled with people and knowledgeable about the work.
- Ensure that crew leaders aren't working from a personal agenda.
- Encourage workers to leave personal agendas in the parking lot.
- Let each person participate in decisions involving her and her work.
- Be generous with praise.
- Don't overlook errors; point them out and learn from them.
- Embrace a lifelong learning philosophy.

Taking a Teamwork Approach

In their book, *The Wisdom of Teams*, authors Jon Katzenbach and Douglas Smith list the following five "common sense" findings about teams in an organization:[3]

1. *A demanding performance challenge tends to create a team.* The hunger to succeed builds unity far better than special incentives or team-building exercises.

2. *The disciplined application of "team basics" is often overlooked.* The basics include size, purpose, goals, skills, approach, and accountability.

3. *Opportunities for team importance exist in all parts of the organization.*

4. *Teams at the top are the most difficult.* The ingrained indi-

vidualism of senior people can conspire against teams at high executive levels.

5. *Most organizations intrinsically prefer individual over group (team) accountability.* Our culture emphasizes individual accomplishments and makes us uncomfortable trusting our career aspirations to outcomes dependent on the performance of others.

Katzenbach and Smith also discovered some "uncommon sense" findings, including the fact that many of the highest performing groups never actually think of themselves as a team. They also found that companies with strong performance standards seem to spawn more "real teams" than companies that promote working groups per se—and that teams are the primary unit of performance in an increasing number of organizations.

Again and again, studies demonstrate that people working together outperform the same number of individuals acting independently. This is especially true when the objective requires a variety of skills and experiences.

Even with the proven success of such alliances, however, many people remain reluctant to join or work within a team. Their reasons include:

- "The meetings are unproductive."
- "Too much time is spent complaining."
- "I believe in individual responsibility."
- "I really don't trust other people."
- "What good are our work decisions? Management will do what they want anyway!"

Fortunately, businesses—and their employees—are discovering the value of teamwork as they move toward flattened organizational structures (as opposed to traditional hierarchical structures), with some decision-making authority spread to lower and lower levels.

Self-managed teams are demonstrating that when the basis for reward is the combined effort rather than individual contribution, participants share knowledge, skills, and ideas to the benefit of all. However, when the basis for reward is the individual effort only, internal competition takes over. In a culture of internal competition, success secrets are guarded, skills are not passed on to co-workers, and ideas are not shared.

For teamwork to be effective, it must be activated not only at the micro-level— among employees at the front line—but also at the macro-level, where management meets.

Unless workers see themselves as part of the organization's team (partners of management), the cooperative spirit will be still-born, and the old spirit of internal competition will flourish. Such internal rivalry is deadly to an organization's ability to fully compete externally.

Military Takes a Teamwork Approach

The United States military, in conjunction with its coalition forces throughout the world, emphasizes the importance of teamwork among its various branches. As we watched daily television war briefings by General Brooks on the war in Iraq in 2003, we noticed that he always attributed successes to the "people," not to the technology. He acknowledged that the technology was the best in the world, but emphasized that it was people working together that made the technology effective.

What General Brooks did was the first step toward building a culture of success: he recognized the importance of the people in his organization. Later that same year, in an interview with Army General Tommy Franks, we heard him say:

> We know that the most capable armed forces in the world are part of this coalition. And if you take the most capable forces in the world, equip them with the right kind of equipment, and put them in motion with a very flexible plan, the outcome is not in doubt.[4]

Of course, that type of strategy takes a capable leader with a culture of success vision. When organizations combine leadership, teamwork, a flat organizational structure, and a well-thought-out but flexible plan, a winning outcome is guaranteed.

Where did the seeds of this change in our traditionally hierarchial military culture originate? With the late Elliott Jaques, known for introducing the concept of business culture in his book, *The Changing Culture of a Factory.*[5] Jaques was also honored by General Colin Powell on behalf of the Joint Chiefs of Staff of the U.S. Armed Forces for "his outstanding contribution in the field of military leadership theory and instruction to all the service departments of the United States and their succeeding generations of officers and men." [6]

Jaques dared to declare that armies have too many levels. Deputies, assistants, and executive officers abound, he lamented. "There is confusion of command at enlisted level, because of uncertainty as to where among NCOs [Non-Commissioned Officers] and junior officers, true first-line command accountability for troops resides."[7]

When Jaques's ideas were rebuffed, he challenged military organizations to a mock war in Louisiana, between his flattened organization and their hierarchical one. The flattened organization won every time. It's a powerful testimony to teamwork, especially as teamwork is needed perhaps more in the military than anywhere else. There is very little margin for error or change during a war.

Measuring the Culture

Once an organization has reduced or eradicated internally competitive strategies, individual feelings of value to the organization will rise. Measure that sense of personal value and you can accurately assess the firm's ability and efficiency to succeed at quality and productivity.

Appendix B contains a chart which reports the results of the Denison Culture Study on how culture impacts the bottom line. This is an excellent example of how important it is to measure culture changes so you can see the positive return on your investment.

In an attempt to examine the culture, we divided a 3,000-person workforce into 19 stratified groups (i.e., management, clerical, shop people, etc.), who were asked to rate their perceived value to the company from 1 (low) to 10 (high) on the following question: "How important do you feel you are to this company?"

A low measure of a group's perceived "value" predicts their low level of interest in quality and productivity.

A high measure predicts a high interest in their work efforts—an expression of "intrinsic" interest in their responsibilities and associated "high quality" capabilities. The higher bars reflect the number of decisions in which workers feel involved. The higher the perceived involvement level, the higher the predicted score on an individual's sense of value to any environment. It's a finding based on pure cause and effect reasoning.

As you may suspect, in the results (see Figure 2.1), the higher values reflect managers, and the lower values, workers. After receiving that report card, the company invested the next three years in building everyone's value to the company.

A culture of success grows in an atmosphere where people at every level feel important to the organization. It's true in businesses, government, health care, athletics, and education.

Figure 2.1

How important do you feel you are to this company?

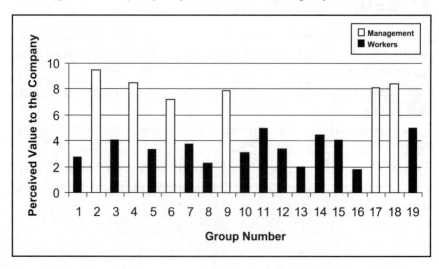

Managers As Coaches

Managers need to convert from their police role to a team leadership role (from "watchdog" to "coach") where they lead initiatives to remove barriers and set an example for others.

Some leaders are willing to make the transition, others are not. Moving to a culture of success can be a frightening prospect for a manager untrained in such systems and not familiar with the behaviors associated with a radical change. As one supervisor noted, "I've been asked to train my staff to make their own decisions, but I feel I'm working myself out of a job."

Which is a true statement. We have somehow vastly underestimated the leadership potential of the average worker, and when companies recognize that fact, they greatly reduce the size of middle management. The good news is that managers who promote change with enthusiasm are either promoted or quickly snapped up by other companies looking for agents of innovation. It is the "I hate this but I'm doing it anyway" supervisor who is left out in the cold.

What about employees? They are also in for a surprise. Accountability, when put in place, no longer allows for a "victim mentality." Since there is no scapegoat, they can no longer pass their responsibilities to a higher level. For everyone, "The buck stops here!"

One for All, and All for One

As we said at the beginning of this chapter, the process begins with developing a vision to which everyone has input. From this shared vision, leaders can set the wheels of change in motion and move from being the watchdog to being the coach. Along with the coach, the team members share in the decision process, will take pride in their work, and as a result produce a higher quality product or service. Soon, the transformation from a traditional management culture to a culture of success will become apparent as the environment of internal competition becomes one of internal cooperation.

Building an environment where trust, respect, and cooperation can flourish takes time, but in the end, your organization will be able to survive and compete in the marketplace.

You will have a culture of success!

Key Concepts

1. In a culture of success, everyone is intrinsically concerned about the success of others.

2. The foremost trait of a culture of success is communication based on trust.

3. Develop a shared vision by defining together why the organization exists and writing a mission statement everyone believes in.

4. When cooperation replaces internal competition good things will happen.

5. A team made up of brilliant individuals each trying to outshine each other quickly becomes a team of brilliant losers.

6. It is not work that burns people out; it is frustration frequently introduced by the boss, system, policies, or work environment.

7. Chemistry develops when people begin to enjoy doing things together and accomplishing things in groups.

8. Many of the highest performance groups never actually think of themselves as a team.

9. People working together historically outperform the same number acting independently.

10. Leaders can shift from watchdog to coach by involving workers in day-to-day decisions.

Things To Do Now

1. Start addressing these questions:
    - How can we build communication based on trust?
    - How can we develop trust in a shared fate?
    - How can leaders shift from watchdog to coach?
2. Share results and arrange meetings to formulate a mission statement that everyone believes in.
3. Look for examples of internal competition across departments and divisions. Meet with all levels of workers and management to determine ways to move from internal competition to team based cooperation.
4. Do more listening, less talking.
5. Consider putting teams together to self-manage tasks. Be prepared to address common reluctancies.
6. Focus work groups on a single agenda.
7. Decide together how the work will be divided and accomplished.
8. Supply sufficient meaningful work.
9. Be generous with praise.
10. Don't overlook errors; point them out and learn from them.

3 POTHOLES TO AVOID

Why do improvement programs fail so frequently? Usually because such programs are created and implemented without regard to the underlying culture.

"I can feel it!" visitors often say when they enter an organization where a culture of success is present. Visitors to the Saturn plant in Tennessee had that feeling. From the inception of the Saturn plant, there were two guiding beliefs:

1. People will support what they help to create.
2. People need to be involved in the decisions affecting them.[1]

Shared vision shows the strength of an empowering strategy and the impact of empowerment on its people's behavior. A system that places individuals in a shared decision-making position is poised to deliver the superior products and services necessary to stay competitive. An organization that ignores the underlying culture, will not have the same opportunities for success. In this chapter we will focus on common "potholes" to avoid on the road to creating a culture of success.

Not a Quick Fix

Organizations planning to move to a culture of success need to understand they are embarking on a long journey. This is no easy task in a world that clamours for instant gratification—internet, fastfood, express mail. We've grown accustomed to instant satisfaction. If an organization can get beyond the quick fix syndrome and begin to make believers of skeptics by "staying the course," anything is possible.

Since both time and capital are required to introduce a culture of success, and since there may be no measurable bottom-line results for a long time, the "budget gods" (those who allocate the resources) typically pull the plug and vote to abort the mission before it has had adequate time to develop.

Poor work practices, mistrust between management and labor, and numerous other "bad things" didn't happen overnight—and they won't be fixed overnight either.

Just as the journey of a thousand miles must start with the first step, so it is with this bold new adventure.

Shared values are what helps organizations gain strength. When employees know their firm's vision, and what standards they are to uphold, they begin to make decisions that support those standards and feel an important part of the organization. As corporate culture experts Terrence Deal and Allan Kennedy put it:

> They are motivated because life in the company or organization has meaning for them.[2]

The Bankruptcy of Bureaucracy

Someone once defined bureaucracy under communism in the USSR as, "I pretend to work, and you pretend to pay me." Unfortunately, this is a mode of operation to which far too many organizations subscribe. Bureaucracies are not only sluggish, secretive, and characterized by decisions made behind closed doors, they've also been declared the "enemy of a healthy workplace."[3]

> Bureaucracy is the art of making the possible, impossible.
>
> —Javier Pascual Salcedo

When workers aren't involved in the decision-making process—and especially when decisions being made directly affect their lives—how can you expect cheerful compliance? Competitive incentive systems so often found in the workplace understandably lead to open conflict and destructive competition.

How can you know if you are dealing with a bureaucratic culture?

Here are some of the telltale signs:

- Too many approvals and signatures required—very little empowerment.
- Avoidance of accountability—management always able to "blame someone."
- A "cover your backside at all costs" attitude.
- Create activity and never mind the results.
- Slow, unresponsive answers to customer complaints.
- Employees "lumped together" and referred to as "they."
- Very little cooperation among departments—each is a world of its own.
- Extensive paperwork, backed up by a massive and complex computer system (often obsolete, inadequate, and not user-friendly).
- Innovation and creativity are discouraged. The status quo is celebrated.

The Pitfalls of Mass Production

The apparent success of American mass production techniques, exemplified by Henry Ford's assembly line, seems to vindicate autocratic management.

The idea behind the concept was to divide up the labor tasks and simplify them so that line workers didn't have to think. All they had to do was pop on hubcaps as the chassis rolled down the assembly line, turn this screw three rotations to the right, and insert this panel into the appropriate slot. In glorifying the assembly line, American industry unknowingly devalued the American worker and destroyed the tradition of craftsmanship. Only now are we waking up to the fact that the mass production methods which we embraced for much of this century are no longer efficient. It has taken an onslaught of quality merchandise from societies in which craftsmanship has survived to convince us that the American way isn't necessarily the best way.

> Good leaders make people feel that they're at the very heart of things, not at the periphery. Everyone feels that he or she makes a difference to the success of the organization. When that happens people feel centered and that gives their work meaning.
>
> **— Warren Bennis, Ph. D.**

The Wrong Incentive

At a steel firm where we served as consultants not long ago, three shifts produced steel bars, and a monetary incentive rewarded the shift producing the greatest quantity with the best quality.

The idea was to stimulate and improve human performance, but it didn't work. Instead of cooperating, each group became involved in sabotaging the ability of the other shifts to do well. The rule of the game as perceived by the workforce was not to produce a quality product, but to do better than the other shifts.

Based on a recommendation from the actual workers, we altered the incentive plan to one based on the total productivity and quality of all three shifts as compared with the previous month. Almost instantly, people began working more cooperatively together, and quality and productivity improved. The new system rewarded cooperation; the old system rewarded competition.

Conditioned to Compete

During each of the more than 1,000 seminars we have presented around the country, we conduct a simple test designed to determine the cooperative or competitive nature of an audience. We place a sentence on an overhead projector and ask participants to count the number of times the letter "F" appears:

> FINISHED FILES ARE THE RESULT OF
> YEARS OF SCIENTIFIC STUDY COMBINED
> WITH THE EXPERIENCE OF MANY YEARS

No matter how we set up the situation, we find it impossible to stimulate real enthusiasm amongst audience members. Participants work individually and do not help one another.

Why? Because they've been asked by a leader to do a task for which they have no ownership. Their goal isn't to do well or be efficient, but to get the leader off their backs. This simple quiz brings out strong competitive traits verifying that we are conditioned to compete. The results? Poor. No one cares; quality runs about fifty percent.

After the evaluation, we ask, "Did you do your best?" The answer is always, "Yes." Yet they perform relatively poorly, some reporting only half of the "F" letters in the sentence.

Their conditioned response is much like Lucy talking with Charlie Brown in the *Peanuts* cartoon about the report due in school the next day. They've been asked to write, "What I Did on My Summer Vacation."

Lucy inquires, "What are you going to say?"

Charlie Brown expounds how his family visited the Grand Canyon and took a lot of photos, went to Disneyland, and saw a live rodeo in Wyoming.

Lucy looks at him rather incredulously and exclaims, "You didn't do any of those things!"

Charlie glances back at Lucy and laments, "I know, but I've been around long enough to know what sells."

As consultants, we see audiences give the same kind of response in the first round of our "F" quiz. But we get different results on a second round, after participants are instructed to work together and help each other. The reaction is almost instantaneous. The noise and enthusiasm intensifies as individuals enjoy the teamwork. We finally have to shout above the noise, "Please stop working now!"

The lesson learned: by changing the culture from one of competition to one of cooperation you can achieve higher quality and spark real enthusiasm in your organization.

Culture Quiz

When do people develop a sense of "ownership" of their task?

When they work together!

When is there enthusiasm for work?

When they work together!

When is work fun?

When they work together!

When do people not need to be watched to do their job?

When they work together!

When is the attention span for a task adequate to produce excellence?

When they work together!

When do people care about quality?

When they work together!

Key Concepts

1. Improvement programs often fail because they ignore the underlying culture.

2. Changing to a culture of success requires time and financial commitment. Just as the problems did not occur overnight, they cannot be solved instantly.

3. Bureaucracy results from internal competition and not involving workers in the decision-making process.

4. Mass production (assembly lines) devalued the labor force and removed quality craftsmanship from products and services.

5. Incentive programs that focus on internal competition instead of internal cooperation usually result in poor quality of products and services.

6. Leadership must "instruct" the workforce to work together and help each other.

Things To Do Now

1. Reduce telltale signs of a bureaucratic environment, such as too many signatures required and little cooperation between departments.

2. Allow people to work together; it will help them develop a sense of ownership of their task.

3. Provide the long-term financing (budget) and resource commitment needed to fund the movement to a culture of success.

4. Look for signs of internal competition and meet with those involved to determine how best to cooperate and work together.

5. Review incentive programs to see if some are promoting internal competition instead of cooperation for better quality product or service.

4 BARRIERS TO CHANGE

Many obstacles block your road to creating a culture of success. Change is frightening for many people, especially those who have seen management fail at prior change attempts. Before you leap into any culture change, you should know the organizational, environmental, and behavioral impacts of navigating a cultural change. In this chapter you will learn about the common barriers to change and how they might impact your efforts to create a culture of success.

The Informal Organization

All organizations have both formal and informal structures that define relationships among the people in that organization. The formal organization is what appears on the organization chart; the official relationships and power structure. The informal organization is formed by people regardless of their official position. They participate in the informal organization to share information, win acceptance, advance their agendas, and build friendships. These people wield significant influence behind the scenes.

The informal organization can influence the formal organization by:

- supporting or resisting change.
- bypassing formalities and cutting through the redtape.
- transmitting valuable information through the grapevine.
- setting the tone or controlling the culture of a workplace.

An effective leader learns to use the informal organization to move the common agenda.[1] So, as you pursue your culture changes, be sure to work *with* the informal organization and take their power into account.

Fear of Change

Following a recent seminar we conducted on "How to Move to a Culture of Success," an executive asked, "Since this approach makes so much sense, why isn't every company doing it?" The answer has to do with fear of change.

For most people, especially entrenched leaders, change is for others—not them. A leader who has reached the top after years of working in a competitive environment would rather not rock the boat. Most of us prefer our own ideas to someone else's. It is human nature to resist anything new or innovative, even when the current situation is barely tolerable. That is why so many opt for the status quo rather than face the challenge of a new idea.

Keeping the Soul Alive

"I can take you out anytime I want to," was a sentiment all too prevalent among managers in the last decade of the twentieth century—a show of power in the ever-spiraling world of downsizing. But each organization has a *heart* and *soul* of its own. When the *soul* is killed, the death of the organization is not far behind. What do we mean by the *soul* of an organization? It is the spirit and force that gives the organization life.

Usually, the on-site manager brings a certain amount of flow and stability to the workplace, allowing people to concentrate on their daily activities. This talent for maintaining workplace harmony is part of the manager's leadership toolkit.

Cost Cutting and Downsizing

Part of the problem is that, in many cases, people sit in offices far removed from the people and workflow, and study the *numbers* in a mystic sense, looking for answers to jump out at them. It is a pretty simple exercise. You start with your gross revenues, subtract any discounts, etc., then start staring at your costs or expenses on the way to reviewing the infamous *bottom line*. Any manager can figure out that if you reduce items on the cost line, the numbers will reflect a larger bottom line. The larger the costs purged, the greater the bottom line. This is pretty much the basis for corporate downsizing.

However, we must be careful when eliminating fat not to cut into the muscle. How many executives know the difference, or take the time to findout? Unnecessary layers of management must go, but not at the expense of losing all of a firm's valuable experience or *killing the spirit* of the organization.

> Listen with your full attention, look for the good in others, have a sense of humor, and say thank you for a job well done.
>
> **—Code of Conduct for JM Smucker, Fortune Magazine's #1 Company to work for.**[2]

Creating a New Flow

New ideas, new organizational structure, as well as new people, all take some getting used to. If all the old comfort symbols are removed, flow stops. It will not start smoothly again until a new flow is established. Without creation of a new spirit, which involves listening in a manner that convinces employees you care, this will not happen.

Why do you think that American workplace morale after downsizing is at rock bottom? Is it any wonder that *trust* has been replaced by fear, and a once-positive attitude is now solely concentrating on getting even?

The howl of the ever-hungry investment community is never quiet. Partnerships with both customers and suppliers grow tenuous at best. When employees see that loyalty is no longer a two-way street, survival becomes the word of the day—survival for one's self, not for the organization. This is entirely different from the cooperative effort required to ensure a company survives.

When employees see fellow workers and management being hit by *friendly fire,* it erodes their ability to focus externally on customers. They are too busy dodging the internal bullets flying around.

What Gets Rewarded, Gets Done

As Peter Drucker has said many times before, *what gets rewarded, gets done*. Employees hear many messages, some mixed, but over time they learn which ones impact their paychecks and which ones do not. Employees quickly figure out the areas that are measured and how they relate to their compensation and focus their attention on those items.

> Instead of managers being a police force, they become leaders who are willing to help remove barriers and set an example for others.

It takes two to six years to change a negative company culture into a positive one. It takes less than five minutes to change from a high-morale, productive workforce dedicated to quality, to a negative one.

A culture of please the customer to please the boss can take root in a microsecond. How does a leader convey what is really important? *What gets rewarded, gets done*. Leaders need to put in place programs that reward positive culture behaviors and make sure that negative culture behaviors do not get rewarded.

The *power* to increase productivity or improve quality is locked in the hearts and minds of those in the workforce. To unlock this power takes an entirely different strategy—one that eludes most managers.

The strategy is simply this: reward positive culture behaviors and you will see positive changes internally, and as a result externally, with customers. *What gets rewarded, gets done*. Note that rewards do not necessarily mean increased compensation. Believe it or not, simple thank you's, pats on the back, and "well done" statements have far more positive, sustained, and motivational power than bonuses or pay increases. Compensation increases alone frequently become entitlements and lose their initial impact over time.

Take Your Power for a Walk

Managers and leaders have power from above—the authority of their position in the organization, and power from below—workers having their own power to withhold effort. What you do with that power directly impacts and shapes the culture.

By getting out of the office and walking around, power (leaders) can have the following positive impact on culture:

1. Recognize jobs well done.

2. Acknowledge things gone wrong with suggestions for improvement and lessons to be learned to prevent repeating the mistake or failure.

3. Demonstrate that the leader cares (enough to be taking time to see what is going on).

4. Most important: the leader sees, hears, feels, and smells firsthand what is actually taking place instead of relying on agenda-laden interpretations from whomever can get in to see the leader first.

The move to a culture of success means: the leader is no longer the agenda, the goals are no longer personal; the shared vision permeates the entire organization.

The real "power" is in the presence and having the authority to make a difference in both results and in the lives of others (she actually noticed what I was doing today).

Environmental Impacts

In transforming a culture, you need to examine the physical, mental, and informational environments present in every organization. Each environment impacts the culture and thus may alter your approach to creating a culture of success. Use the following list of questions for each environment as a guide to your investigation.

Physical Environment

- Is the workspace adequate or does the worker feel trapped or confined? Thoughts flow more freely when the area around us is in flow (a feng shui concept).

- Is the atmosphere conducive to high-energy performance? What about fresh air, temperature, noise, and smell?

- Are the proper equipment and resources provided? Is everything in working order? If not, does the worker have the means to correct it?

Mental Environment

- How would you assess the interaction between the worker's peer group and related supervisors?

- What is the morning ritual? Do they say "Good morning" to each other? Do they smile?

- Is it a workplace with feeling, or is it a sterile, non-caring environment? Is there joy in the workplace? Would you describe the situation as happy or hostile?

Informational Environment

- Is the workforce included or excluded in the flow and availability of company information?

- What is the organization's *compelling story?* Does every associate know and believe in this story?

    Why would a customer want to buy from us?

    Why would someone want to work here?

    Why would a vendor want to supply us?

    Why would someone want to invest in us?

- Are workers pursuing company or individual agendas?

- Do workers feel a part of the organization?

- What are the myths?

- Who are the heroes?

Division of Labor

Let's face it. We've been trapped by tradition. In the United States, under the guise of the historic 1920s scientific management, we have created what is often called "division of labor." Complex tasks are broken down into the smallest increments and assigned to people who do the same basic tasks over and over. The theory is that when workers become very proficient, production will soar. But as we have learned, the workforce soon becomes bored and disengaged from the entire process. Workers lose touch with leadership and work only for pay, not for pride or purpose.

As a natural by-product of the division of labor, the labor movement negotiated written work practices to protect jobs. What was the result? Each worker or service provider was encouraged to do his or her task—certainly not to volunteer or cooperate with other workers to help accomplish the overall objective.

Clearly both sides—management and labor—got it wrong, but for different reasons. And you know what surprised many experts? When they began talking with workers and service providers, they found that these people didn't like the system either.

Leaders who began employing strategies such as "managing by walking around" and communicating directly with workers and associates were amazed by the results. For the first time, they saw that employees felt that their opinions counted. Leaders and workers found that joining forces, cross-training, and cooperating made work more enjoyable and lent a sense of self-accomplishment.

The Burden of Leadership

Where does change begin? With leadership. That's where the vision is created and communicated. But how do you "lead" change? Selecting the right leadership style may be your best first step toward changing the culture in your organization.

History documents many successful leadership models, each with unique characteristics best suited for specific situations. Leadership by example is perhaps the strongest leadership style. Napolean and Patton led by example and were popular with their troops because they led them into battle, but not all leadership situations occur in such dramatic situations as found on a battlefield.

Leadership by making difficult decisions at difficult times, having good judgment, and being able to "stay the course" over a long period of time is another strong leadership model. Abraham Lincoln exemplifies this leadership style. This is the leadership style required to change an organization's culture.

> Give your subordinates a fair chance with equal freedom and opportunity for success.
>
> — Abraham Lincoln

Abraham Lincoln demonstrated leadership qualities throughout his life, but only when the future of our nation was at stake did he demonstrate the true depth of his ability to cope and use wisdom in his judgments and decisions.

Lincoln had to find a way to preserve the nation. The situation demanded decisive action on complex issues. Neither popular nor understood, Lincoln fought the politics of the North as much as the army of the South. He had few, other than his immediate family, rooting for his success. However, he was not seeking personal success. He focused on a single vision: preserve the nation.

Lincoln did not hide in the solace of his office or behind his Cabinet. He went into the battlefield to talk to generals and troops, and share his vision.

Despite the heavy burdens, he retained his humor, continued to be a people person, and never considered "growing an ego" to fit his large physical frame.

A man of high values and integrity, Lincoln believed so much in the democratic principles on which this nation was founded that he found the courage to make difficult and oftentimes unpopular decisions to save the union. Despite extreme political pressure, he was able to sort out the facts and stick to them. In the end, he made the supreme sacrifice—his life.

Today, Lincoln personifies the "burden of leadership." A culture change demands a strong leader who will bear the burden of leadership, someone who can make tough decisions in difficult times, exercise good judgment, and be able to "stay the course" over a long period of time.

The Nature of Organizations

Another common barrier to culture change is best described by psychologist Harry Levinson. Levinson detailed what happens to large and previously highly successful enterprises that have been having problems adapting to changing educational circumstances. He lays blame on the organization's inability to think creatively, and denial—"the inability to accept facts and do something about them."[3]

Levinson lists the following five fundamental truths about organizations:

1. All organizations recapitulate the family structure and the behavioral practices of the culture in which they are embedded.

2. All animals and human beings differentiate themselves into in-groups and out-groups and develop what might be called an in-group narcissism: the "we-they" phenomenon.

3. All organizations, by definition, being made up of people, are living organisms. They have developmental histories and evolve adaptive patterns that deal with different levels of complexity.

4. All living organisms experience continuous change, both within themselves and within their environment.

5. All groups follow a leader. Different groups at different times require alternate styles of leadership, but the founding leader's policies, practices, and organizational structure frequently endure.

Why are these five fundamental truths important? Many corporate problems stem directly from underestimating or misunderstanding the natural factors that impact organizations. By taking the time to study your existing culture and the natural patterns of organizations in general, you will be better equipped to navigate and bring about a cultural change.

Win–Win Strategies

Far too often, when a subordinate asks, "Why?" the response is, "Because I am your supervisor. That's why!" (Or at home, "Because I am your parent. That's why!")

Which is a fine response for a win-lose arena, but completely unacceptable for a win-win culture of success environment. To create a win-win cooperative atmosphere, consider the following:

- Turn disagreements into opportunities for discussions.
- Define a common agenda, and use that shared vision or common ground to negotiate solutions that work for all (win-win).
- Make sure that a partnership of "equals" truly exists at all levels.
- Keep the lines of communication open at all times.
- Focus more on similarities and less on differences.

Don't Delay, Involve Employees Today

Delaying change on the basis that now isn't the "right time" can have serious consequences. Leaders of companies like IBM and Sears brought in outsiders to turn their fortunes around to accelerate change. These companies and many others had lost market share to competitors who chose a direction of "people growth" strategies through involvement and teamwork. Even the more traditional companies are starting to fight back using these new approaches.

The central difference between enterprises that survive and those that fail is employee involvement.

Wal-Mart is a stellar example. They used employee motivation techniques to become a formidable player in the competitive retail market. In a recent Wal-Mart employee newsletter, an employee was *honored* (front-page photograph and personal information) for suggesting a change he believed would improve productivity. The article mentioned that the suggested change cost Wal-Mart over $5,000 and did not work, but that the firm wanted to applaud the employee for trying to improve a situation!

Where does the change to a culture that involves employees begin? In one word—*leadership.* That's where the vision is both created and communicated. At first, new ideas have to be "sold" because no one is quite sure of the new strategy, but that phase does not need to last long.

"Shared vision" must become more than a glib phrase. Are you ready to spend six months seriously revising your mission statement and strategic plan so that they reflect input from every member of your organization? A tactical "action plan" is hollow rhetoric unless mutually developed by everyone involved.

Case Study: Shareholder Value Creation

From 1983 to his retirement, the chairman of Lloyds Bank TSB, Sir Brian Pitman, led the bank through a company turnaround, increased its market capitalization forty-fold and, in the process, led a transformation of the company's culture. He convinced his management team that to achieve return on equity required a culture shift. His term was "shareholder value creation."

> For people to be truly committed to a strategy of shareholder value creation, they have to believe in it... You can't impose a mindset on people. [Commitment] emerges from a learning process [during] which they become persuaded that an objective is worthwhile, and then apply their talents to realizing it.
>
> The process often involves heated debate; indeed, I found that disagreement is key to getting agreement. Without disagreement, people will simply fall into line with no real commitment to the program. I simply cultivated an environment that encouraged — not required — inquiry. And, not surprisingly, people came up with all kinds of bright ideas for achieving our aim. Intelligent people, presented with an intellectual challenge, become deeply engaged in the endeavor. Indeed, the intellectual journey was an exciting one for all of us."[4]

Who Is The Real Owner?

We hear much about "ownership," but how is it stimulated? How is it produced?

At an awards banquet we recently attended, the organization's leader was eager to announce the successful completion of a monumental task—their operation's mission statement. "There are three people who have invested their time and energy with me for two years to create this statement, and I want you to meet them," he declared. Three senior managers stepped forward to receive impressive plaques on which the mission statement had been engraved.

What's wrong with that scenario? The company leader was sincere, but his approach ensured that only he and the three individuals he honored would leave the room with an intrinsic sense of ownership.

What should he have done? He should have arranged for a representative from each division in the company to be involved throughout the process. He should have shared frequently updated working copies with every employee until the mission statement was completed, and made a point of thanking everyone.

When buy-in occurs, miracles begin to happen. As one manager told us, "I just stay in the background and help resolve problems only when I am asked. Our work teams know the objectives because they helped develop them. And they love the responsibility."

Douglas McGregor, who was a highly regarded management professor at M.I.T., agrees. He stated, "We have learned that, if we push decision-making down in an organization as far as we possibly can, we tend to get better decisions, people tend to grow and to develop more rapidly, and they are motivated more effectively."[5]

Don't be discouraged by barriers of tradition, opposing forces, or a natural resistance to change. What seems like a mountain of granite will be reduced to stepping-stones when tackled by a team.

Key Concepts

1. Barriers to change can undermine your culture change efforts.

2. Fear of change is a common barrier, especially at the top.

3. Downsizing and cost-cutting programs often work against the culture of success principles.

4. New organizational structures usually mean the removal of old ways, which stops the normal flow of an organization.

5. What gets rewarded, gets done.

6. Physical, mental, and informational environmental impacts can be obstacles on the road to a culture change.

7. Division of labor approach causes internal competition and managers to become a police force—both work against creating a culture of success.

8. An organization's spirit is the force that gives it life (motivation, enthusiasm, flow, and stability) and must be kept alive during the culture change.

9. Changing a negative culture to a positive one can take two to six years, but it takes less than five minutes to change a high-morale, productive workforce to a negative one.

10. Be sure to involve employees in the culture change, but remember that change begins with the leadership.

11. Abraham Lincoln's "stay the course" leadership is an effective leadership style for changing an organization's culture.

12. Take the "informal organization" into account as you plan for culture changes.

Things To Do Now

1. Eliminate unnecessary layers of management without killing the spirit.

2. Take care not to remove all of the old comfort symbols. If old symbols must be replaced, be sure to have the new symbols created by all levels in your organization.

3. Manage by walking around and communicating directly with workers and associates—it gets results.

4. Join forces with workers, cross-train, and cooperate.

5. Promote change with enthusiasm.

6. Work to eliminate the victim mentality.

7. Make disagreements opportunities for discussion, and failure an opportunity for learning.

8. Keep lines of communication open at all times.

9. If you are a leader, create and communicate the vision.

10. Push decision-making downward in an organization as far as you can.

5 WAKE-UP CALL

Are the signs of needed change all around you, but no one else seems to notice? How do you go about giving others a "wake-up call?" You certainly cannot force-feed a culture change to fellow leaders or staff. In this chapter, we explore the challenges of being the change-leader.

Leading Change

Have you ever tried to help someone who does not want assistance? It is virtually impossible. People refuse help for a variety of reasons—including the fact that they are unaware they need help.

Here is how it works in many organizations: Managers who do not communicate with others in the organization get upset with the brave soul who tries to let them know what's happening. They literally "shoot the messenger." The manager often sees the "messenger" as a complainer, instead of as someone trying to help. Over time people learn to avoid these managers and "let them find out on their own."

> Time spent with fellow workers is as valuable an investment as time spent with customers.

Here is a simple test you can use to determine the awareness of a manager or supervisor. Ask: "How are things on the floor?" Substitute the term "floor" for any similar phrase for your organization (such as ward for a hospital). If the answer is usually: "I don't know, but I will check and be right back." Be wary, as you may be working with a manager who seldom leaves the office to "walk the floor" or to communicate with others.

Managers can learn remarkable things when they get out of the office and "walk the floor." Only by "being there" can we take preventative action or see what needs attention. If what is taking place is healthy, you are in a position to recognize good performance. By making the effort to "be there" you show you care and that what each person is contributing is important to you and to the organization.

Develop a culture to solve problems, not delegate blame. If difficult issues are handled fairly, people will seek you out and tell you about them.

The Fear Factor

Communication and trust rise and fall together inside an organization. Nothing will destroy trust faster than fear. Employees may be fearful of failure, of retribution by supervisors, of voicing an opinion, or of change itself. These fears are what we call the "fear factor." The fear factor stifles communication, which leads to a lack of trust and, before you know it, the doors to a culture of success close.

Ken Kivenko, former president and CEO of Canada Marconi Company explained it this way:

> Fear of failure, fear of supervisors, fear of voicing an opinion, and fear of change are the chief enemies of timely action and flexibility. Until fear is minimized or eliminated, experimentation with new concepts will not become commonplace.[1]

How do you know if you have a "fear factor" problem? Look for these telltale signs:

- Information is often hoarded as a source of power, not shared.
- Few questions are asked at meetings.
- Memos and e-mails are carefully scripted to justify one's actions and defend one's positions.

You can easily see how such actions work against the success of an organization. But how can you reverse such actions? You must look at the cause of the fear—look for the fear factor that is driving that destructive behavior.

Moving from a traditional culture whose traditions embraced command and control autocratic management, where trust may or may not have been the norm, must start by finding ways to drive out fear. By driving out fear the level of trust goes up. As the level of trust increases, the level of communication goes up.

You can greatly reduce the fear factor by:

- Addressing rumors immediately.
- Providing avenues for employees to communicate.
- Being easily accessible.
- Carefully listening to others in your organization.
- Asking questions and involving others in the decision making process.
- Recognizing and rewarding outstanding performance.
- Allowing failures to become learning experiences.
- Driving out "victim thinking."
- Installing accountability at all levels, starting with management.
- Celebrating the team's successes.

Starting the Transformation

In order for a transformation to a culture of success to occur; there must be commitment on the part of the CEO—the leader of the organization. Lee Thayer, who spent his career as a professor of organizational development, is one of the most effective consultants in helping a CEO turn an organization around. When Lee receives a 100% commitment to change from the CEO, he will guarantee success. What he will not guarantee is how long it will take.

How long will it take? On average, we have found that it takes two to six years to change the leadership style of an organization from autocratic to democratic; depending upon how deeply the

> "If we don't change our direction, we're likely to end up where we're headed."
> —Ancient Chinese Proverb

old system is ingrained into your current culture.

To change the *culture* of an organization, the values that drive the organization (the beliefs) must be reviewed.

If there is a unwillingness to change beliefs; the behavior of the leadership will not change either. Without a change in behavior, there is not change in the results we get—the culture will stay the same.

To effectively change the culture, the leadership may have to be changed or at least helped with guidance from the outside. What must take place is a movement from *what's in it for me* to *shared fate*. It sounds simple, but a move to shared fate requires hard work and a deep commitment.

Not everyone will be able to make this transformation. Training, peer pressure, and outside facilitation are all tools that should be used. In the end, some won't make it. They must find other organizations where their "old style" is still acceptable.

David Kearns, former CEO of Xerox, explains why the role of the leader in developing a culture of success is so important:

> Developing a quality culture in an organization most often requires a dramatic change in the way people in the organization see the world and their roles within it. It requires that they think and act differently.
>
> The extent of the needed change in culture can be traumatic for any organization and like all change, it is often actively resisted by many. This is why the role of the leader in developing a quality culture is so critical.[2]

Management Trends

Without question, as we start the twenty-first century, management trends toward improved democratic systems of leadership seem to be the best strategy for continued economic survival. Traditional 1950s dictatorial styles of leadership must yield to more effective systems of shared decision making.

During the last half of the twentieth century, Japan emerged as a world economic power. The secret to Japan's success was a unique Japanese management style based on the quality principles of quality movement leaders such as Deming and Juran. Appendix A, "A Quick Course on Quality," provides you with more in-depth information on the quality movement and its impact on work culture.

In the years since, global management trends continue to follow the core Japanese management principles. Popular trends such as "Six Sigma" (data-driven quality management) have their roots in these Japanese management principles. We have found them to be vital guidelines for leaders pursuing a culture change. Here is a brief summary of the key principles and how they relate to creating a culture of success.

1. Shared Decision Making

"Ringi" is the Japanese process for reaching decisions by consensus. This principle ensures that all people who will be involved in implementing a decision have a say in making that decision in the first place.

The nature of sharing in the overall decision making process provides a powerful sense of ownership (buy-in). Those who are part of the effort look forward to their work and care passionately about the future of the company.

2. Strong Internal and External Relationships

"Keiretsu" refers to a uniquely Japanese form of corporate organization. A keiretsu is a grouping or family of affilitated companies that form a tight-knit alliance to work toward each other's mutual success.

The power of a management and workforce that shares the *vision* of their company is mighty, and, it multiplies when coupled with a cooperative relationship with customers and suppliers. We believe it is the only way to effectively compete in the current economic climate.

3. Incremental Continuous Improvement

"Kaizen" is Japanese for "change for the better" or "improvement." Kaizen is a business philosophy of continuous team-based improvement activity. In other words, the plan to strategically develop a working system to increase productivity and quality is never-ending.

In companies where we have personally been involved for lengthy periods, we have noted that maintaining a program of continuous improvement is directly related to the sustaining nature of quality and productivity. The need to constantly review and improve the systems of world-class companies is continual.

Case Study: Marion Correctional Facility

Here is a dramatic example of culture change that took place at the Marion Medium Security Correctional Institution for Men in Marion, Ohio. During a recent visit to the institution, Head Warden Chris Money told the story of the condition (culture) of the prison back in 1996 when she and Deputy Warden Cliff Smith first arrived.

Fear was rampant among the inmates. There was very little trust among any of the people within the organization. It was a dangerous place. In some cases, inmates were continuing their criminal activity inside the prison including drug dealing, extortion, and knifing. It was not a culture of rehabilitation but a culture of retribution and fear. Inmates just hoped to survive, serve their time, and get released. Unfortunately, no time or effort had been successfully invested to prepare them for the outside world when they were released. The cycle of crime and punishment just continued.

Wardens Money and Smith knew that these behaviors had to change in order for them to make progress. They also knew that behaviors are driven beliefs. They started the change by installing faith-based activities to start changing the beliefs of some of the inmates. The faith-based activities came from a variety of faiths including Christianity, Judaism, and Islam. Starting with a core of 88 of the over 1500 inmates in a special environment where their spirituality and commitment to their faith could be practiced, the culture slowly evolved as trust started to grow. Trust and communication grew together. Involvement of the inmates, at all levels, has become key to the change from a "prison" to a "community." Seven years later, Wardens Money and Smith report that over half of the inmates believe in a "faith-based" system.

A faith-based strategy worked in this context. If such a dramatic culture change can occur in a correctional facility, surely we can define other appropriate and workable culture change techniques in our schools, our companies, and our communities. It starts with commitment and careful selection of change strategies. It starts at the top and it involves everyone in the organization.

It's Not a Contest

Many companies fail to realize that any system that encourages internal competition is a major departure from the objective.

True teamwork is highlighted by total internal cooperation of all employee groups, including those in management. The intent of the team-structured workplace is to eliminate—or at least greatly diminish—in-house competition.

Since product and service quality won't take shape without worker cooperation, moving toward a true team environment and formally analyzing the systems, together offer the best way to achieve a culture of success.

Futuristic management thinking will become a more complex balancing act. Management will continue to be held accountable for results. Management must also be capable of higher strata thinking, which means dealing with more complexity into a longer future time frame than in the past. Being able to adapt to changing market conditions while being flexible to accommodate the emergence of greater employee involvement and shared decision-making will characterize the successful leaders of the future.

Management needs to approach their challenge with the same enthusiasm as William Eaton, an executive at Levi Strauss, who says:

On a day-to-day basis, my passion comes from backing people's efforts, getting them what they need to do the job, educating them, and working with them as a member of the team.[3]

Now, that's a wake-up call for success!

Key Concepts

1. You cannot force-feed culture changes.

2. Communication and trust rise and fall together in an organization.

3. Drive out the fear factors to see the level of trust increase, and with it, the level of communication rise.

4. The CEO or organization leader must be committed to the transformation or you will not be able to move to a culture of success.

5. Culture changes take from two to six years, although a traumatic or sudden event can force a culture shift in a shorter period of time.

6. To change the culture of an organization, the values that drive the organization (beliefs) must be reviewed and participants must be willing to change their beliefs.

7. Certain Japanese business principles provide excellent guidelines for building a culture of success.

8. Team-structured work practices minimize the destructive forces of internal competition.

9. Autocratic, top-down leaders are ill-equipped for futuristic managerial thinking.

10. The new leadership style embraces a passion for coaching, teaching, and supporting staff members.

11. A management system based on "updated" world-class standards is an excellent way to stay in sync with proven management trends.

Things To Do Now

1. Work with all levels of line and staff, offering the same level of caring and sharing once reserved for customers.

2. Handle troubling issues quickly and fairly in order to influence others to bring issues to your attention when they can still be nipped in the bud.

3. Supply leadership training based on the quality principles of Deming and Juran (see Appendix A for more details).

4. Strive for a people-centered leadership style.

5. Consider using ISO-9000 style standards (consistent with your organizational goals) as a method to document progress. For more information, see their website: www.ISO.org.

6. Try using the Baldrige National Quality Award criteria to structure a management and operational system capable of world-class performance. For more information, see their website: www.quality.nist.gov.

6 PEOPLE WANT TO CARE

Why work twelve hour days for a company that does not care about you? That is the question on the minds of many workers today. Workers now have choices—where they work, and how much effort they put into each task performed. It may seem obvious, but if so, why are so many people unhappy at work and so many employers frustrated with poor quality of worker output? This chapter explores the impact employee-employer care has on the success of a culture change, and, ultimately, the success of your organization.

A Two-Way Street

The best way to get workers to care about the success of an organization is to involve them in as many decisions as possible. How is this done? By having leaders visit with employees on every work shift, at their workplace. If possible, such conversations should take place daily.

When leaders demonstrate that kind of personal concern, employees are more than ready to respond positively to the organization's needs.

Two-way streets must not only be built, they must be paved over with mutual respect and trust, and then repaved, so that over time, the road becomes familiar and the new culture ingrained.

Case Study: Empowering Employees

Gregg Foster had reached the No. 2 position in someone else's company. He was restless and wanted to venture out on his own. He finally found his "company"—an eighty-five-year-old iron foundry losing $3 million a year on annualized sales of $4 million. He was drawn to the Elyria Iron Foundry because of his brief experience working at a foundry during college one summer, and because it was located in the area he wanted to live. Plus, it was about all he could afford.

During the next eighteen months of negotiations, Foster watched the economic fortunes of the foundry sink deeper and deeper. Finally, a deal was struck.

Foster immediately shut the plant down and interviewed three hundred "former" employees for potential rehire. He offered jobs to the one hundred candidates with the best performance records, then called them together and announced:

I don't care what you used to do here — it didn't work. As of last Friday, this became a new company, and we will be doing things differently.[1]

Foster not only involved the workers in decision-making from that point onward, but from the president on down he ensured that all managers had a "line job" as well. He also abolished the position of foreman, replacing that position with a section leader who wore the same kind of work clothes as those on the line.

We have seen the operation firsthand, and can testify that Foster's employees are passionate about the company. Nothing speaks louder to their culture of success transformation than the fact that turnover at the foundry is practically zero.

Foster made advocates of his employees. In return, he got a supportive workforce and harmonious labor relations. Plus, his company survived as a profitable operation while ten others around him were going under.

At the end of the first year of this arrangement, Foster implemented a profit-sharing plan that allowed him to cut a modest check for each employee. The union, however, told the workers to return the checks, since the profit-sharing arrangement was not in the union contract. The workers not only ignored this order; they told the union leaders, "This guy's trying to help us. We're going to support him."

Within a few years, annual sales zoomed from $4 million to over $35 million, and because of the uniqueness of his success,

Foster was named one of *Inc.* magazine's "Entrepreneurs of the Year." Here are his eleven personal maxims for success:

1. Take on one problem at a time.
2. Newcomers can effect change easier than incumbents.
3. Job security is an oxymoron.
4. Trust your spouse and ignore your lawyer.
5. Don't let adverse facts stand in the way of a good decision.
6. Trust instincts and react.
7. Look forward; forget the past.
8. Be decisive about decisions on the first day.
9. Embrace change and reward risk.
10. Keep your sense of humor.
11. Have no ego.

Involve the Workers

While interviewing three hundred employees at a large company, we asked, "Are you loyal to the company or to the union?" Many responded, "If I had the opportunity, I would like to be on the company team and the union team."

We found that more than 90% of the employees at that company indicated that they'd like a chance to work with management and identify with the company while still maintaining a relationship with the union.

Clearly, employees want to be involved with the companies that they serve. Companies can greatly benefit from involving their employees in the day-to-day decision making process.

During a visit to Honda of America Manufacturing, we overheard a tour guide mention that during the past decade, the company had set in motion over 10,000 suggestions from individuals and "Quality Circle Teams" which resulted in savings for Honda worth countless millions of dollars.

> The key to satisfaction and motivation is basic human decency. Humans are at least as bright and sensitive as houseplants. Treat them well and they will flourish.
>
> —Joe Anderson, TEC Chair

Another car manufacturer, Toyota of America, at their plant in Georgetown, Kentucky, reported that 97% of its employees participate in the firm's decision-making processes. This is an amazing figure, given that traditional American automotive manufacturing companies, while getting much better, still involve a much smaller percentage of employees to participate in decision-making.

Ideally, 90% of the work-site problems or decisions should be handled by the people at that work-site, leaving management free to concentrate on process planning, strategic development, and execution. That is what we call a culture of success.

The Advantages

Decline in productivity can be traced to environments that condone internal competition.

S. G. "Buck" Rogers, of IBM fame, wrote two books: *The IBM Way* and then, later on, *Getting the Best – Out of Yourself and Others*. The dramatic differences between the two books (old IBM way versus new IBM way) highlight the importance of focusing on people and ridding your organization of internal competition.

A cooperative work environment offers at least four advantages over the traditional "competitive" management style:

1. Speed and flexibility—leaders can move quickly, with flexibility, to meet external competition.

2. Full support from employees—leaders can count on a 100% effort from all employees.

3. Free exchange of ideas—workers exchange ideas with leaders on how to meet new challenges.

4. Open Communication—leaders maintain an open communication forum to avoid misunderstandings.

Overcoming Skepticism

What does a leader do when skepticism breeds a level of resistance difficult to overcome? That's when you enlist outside help. Someone with culture transformation experience in another operation is often in a better position to sell the concept to a variety of stakeholders than someone on the inside. This person needs to work with the leaders and *together* show each of the various interest groups how they—and the organization—will benefit.

> Eventually, the critics realize that a cooperative atmosphere not only returns joy to the workplace, but also increases quality, productivity, and profitability to the organization.

Those who have thrived for years on conflict, strife, and tension won't know what hit them when the troops of the new culture arrive. They'll feel like they've been run over by a steamroller. They will have to either join the ranks, or be treated as relics of a bygone era. Typically, resisters who cannot change choose to leave of their own accord.

Testing the Culture

In our seminars, we ask, "How many of you enjoy going home?" Most people immediately smile and raise their hands. Then we ask, "Do you realize why you feel this way?"

One of the leading reasons people look forward to their family life is that they participate in the decision process at home. Ideally, they view their family life as a team-based environment where open communication without fear of retribution flourishes.

A simple test you can give to any employee is to ask the question, "Do you enjoy going to work?"

In traditional, autocratic arenas, managers usually answer "Yes" and workers answer "No." Why? Because people who share in the decision process look forward to going to work each day, and those who have little input at work dread going to work. This is true at work, at school, or any organization where people establish only extrinsic (money, grades, etc.) motivation for excellence.

When a worker at your organization pulls out a photo of fellow staff or workmates and exclaims, "Here are the people I work with, they're great," you know you are well on the way to your objective.

An employee's training, experience, and competence may say a lot about the individual, but it says nothing about the work environment. The best barometer of the work environment is how people treat each other at work.

When you hear a worker exclaim, "I love what I do!" and then hear someone else say, "Can I help you with that? Together we can get it done right," that's when you know that the gates to a culture of success have swung open.

Key Concepts

1. Success is a two-way street: if you care about your workers and treat them with respect and trust, they will care about the company and produce higher quality products.

2. Participatory decision-making breeds passionate loyalty and profitability.

3. When managers demonstrate true personal concern, employees become more responsive to an organization's needs.

4. Most workers today want to identify with management.

5. At companies with a culture of success, the workforce (not management) tackles at least 90% of the problems that arise.

6. A cooperative working arrangement has at least four advantages over the traditional autocratic management style: speed and flexibility, full support from employees, free exchange of ideas, and open communication.

7. People involved in daily decision-making look forward to going to work every day. Those not involved in decision-making do not enjoy going to work.

8. The best barometer of a healthy work environment is employees who love what they do and care about their co-workers.

Things To Do Now

1. Take on one problem at a time, trust your instincts, keep your ego in check and maintain your sense of humor.

2. Embrace and reward risk.

3. Exhibit decisiveness on your first day on the job.

4. Visit with workers daily on every work shift, on their turf.

5. When you encounter insurmountable skepticism and resistance from the workforce, bring in an outside third-party source or consultant, who can often effect change more easily.

6. Set a goal that 90% of decisions are made by the actual people at the work-site or locale where the decision is needed.

7. Develop opportunities, activities, and events that allow the employees to identify with the company.

8. Get employees involved in cost-saving projects and develop a system to reward them for their efforts.

7 ELIMINATING THE ENEMY WITHIN

Internal competition—the enemy within—is nothing new. All our lives we've been conditioned to compete. At home, parents brag about the son or daughter who is "best." Schools pit students against one another for everything from sports to SAT scores. On the job, various patterns and processes create champions and casualties.

Competitive systems produce negative side effects:

1. Roughly half of the population has to fail or perform at an inferior level for the other half to feel successful.

2. Competition produces winners and losers. Worse, instead of yielding "good losers," it inspires resentful or "get even" behavior.

3. In win/lose arenas, no one lives up to his full potential, because simply "doing better" than someone else is equivalent to winning.

> The focus on competition has always been a formula for mediocrity.
>
> —Daniel Burrus

The "internally competitive culture" continues to undermine organizations large and small—schools, hospitals, public and private, for-profit and not-for-profit organizations.

As Figure 7.1 on the following page illustrates, while many corporations and institutions believe they are headed in the right direction, a dramatic difference exists between an enterprise guided by a team agenda and one driven by individual agendas. As you compare the two diagrams in Figure 7.1, consider which of the two organizations (Team or Individual Agenda) will be more successful?

Figure 7.1

Ownership and Empowerment (Team Agenda)

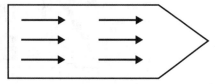

Internal Competition (Individual Agenda)

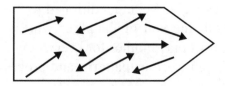

If they were school systems, to which one would you send your child?

The Role of Autocratic Leadership

The cause-effect relationship between autocratic leadership and internal competition is not theory, it is fact. Autocratic leadership stimulates competition and divisiveness among those being led.

To please a domineering leader, employees will do whatever it takes—including pushing co-workers aside to gain favor with the leader.

What is the ultimate result? Individual employees struggling for approval and self-survival who are no longer concerned with excellence. In business, this translates into poor quality of goods and services. The following case study provides a thought-provoking story that illustrates the frequently serious consequences of an autocratic leadership style.

Case Study: Crash and Burn

Melburn McBroom was a domineering boss, with a temper that intimidated those who worked with him. That fact might have passed by unnoticed had McBroom worked in an office or factory, but McBroom was an airline pilot.

One day in 1978, McBroom's plane was approaching Portland, Oregon when he noticed a problem with the landing gear. So McBroom went into a holding pattern, circling the field at a high attitude while he fiddled with the mechanism.

As McBroom obsessed about the landing gear, the plane's fuel gauges steadily approached the empty level, but his copilots were so fearful of McBroom's wrath that they said nothing, even as disaster loomed. The plane crashed, killing ten people.

Today, the story is told as a cautionary tale in the safety training of airline pilots.[1] In 80% of airline crashes, pilots make mistakes that could have been prevented, particularly if the crew worked together more harmoniously. Teamwork, open lines of communication, cooperation, listening, and speaking one's mind are now emphasized in training pilots, along with technical skills.

The cockpit is a microcosm of any working organization. Although lacking the dramatic reality check of an airplane crash, the destructive effects of miserable morale, intimidated workers, and arrogant bosses—or any of the dozens of other permutations of emotional deficiencies in the workplace—can go largely unnoticed by those outside the immediate scene. The costs can be read in signs such as decreased productivity, an increase in missed deadlines, mistakes, and mishaps, and an exodus of employees to more congenial settings.

There is, inevitably, a cost to the bottom line from low levels of emotional intelligence on the job. When it is rampant, companies can "crash and burn."

Time and Place for Both

Traditional systems of management produce a "pick the best and forget the rest" culture that kills morale—a problem compounded when the reward system is based on internal competition. We often think of achievers as self-motivated, goal-driven individuals who would succeed regardless of the obstacles. Yet now we are beginning to understand that motivation depends on the environment in which we find ourselves—it turns us on, or it turns us off.

Autocratic, domineering, controlled atmospheres stifle

achievement, destroy self-worth, diminish morale, and impede human progress. Is there a place for autocratic management? Yes. When an urgent situation requires an immediate response, auto-cratic leadership makes sense, even to subordinates. Most people know the difference.

On the other hand, in a non-crisis day-to-day environment, people functioning in a cooperative, democratic sphere tend to accept the new ideals and objectives and adapt to them with en-thusiasm.

Case Study: Autocratic vs. Democratic Leadership

The New York Times won a record seven Pulitzer prizes under Executive Editor Howell Raines. But, autocratic leadership suc-cesses come with a price tag. For Raines that price was steep, as he was forced to resign from his position. Had Raines been a more democratic leader, employees would have rallied around him when reporter Jayson Blair's fic-tional reporting was exposed. But, as it was, edi-tors had warned Raines who ignored them.

> Managers need to know when and how to be autocratic. There is a time and place for both styles (autocratic and democratic), but people can and should be treated with respect in either leader-ship style.

As the saying goes, there is a time and place for everything. Autocratic lead-ership is necessary in crisis situations. Organizations need strong leaders with good judgment and a grasp of the larger picture to direct workers in a crisis. Newsrooms under deadlines, troops on a battlefield, and a sailing ship in a storm are all good examples of situations that warrant autocratic leadership.

Yet, companies are not democracies. "The line is hazy at best," says Jeff Rich, CEO of Affiliated Computer Services (ACS), a Fortune 500 company based in Dallas with more than 36,000 em-ployees.

Large companies should keep most decisions democratic ex-cept in times of crisis or when there is no consensus, Rich says. "Purely autocratic leaders ultimately become bottlenecks because people learn that the best survival skill is to ask the boss before making a decision."

"People learn to wait for directives from the boss or worse, they become terrified about making the wrong decision," says Rich. "In any case, creativity is discouraged, and the most talented people eventually leave."[2]

Knowing when to be democratic and when to be autocratic may be the determining factor that makes or breaks your culture of success.

Who's the Leader?

In roundtable discussions with corporate leaders we are often asked, "You say that in a culture of success the focus is on everyone being a potential winner—yet only one person can be at the top. How does that work?"

This is a very valid question. In a cooperative organization culture, being at the top is a *shared* experience. Even though one individual may have a special title and responsibilities, team members and the "appointed leader" buy into a single shared vision.

Probably one of the best examples we've run across of this was described by employees at Honda of America Manufacturing:

> Our objective is to work with enthusiasm and quality to make sure that both our team and our leaders look good.

In our experience, as people move to an arena of unity, team members ensure that the leader will not fail. Why?

1. Team members have too much invested personally to allow the venture to collapse.

2. Since there is an equal commitment by all parties, team members pull together for the shared vision to succeed.

In an ideal team environment, if the leader is not "right" for a particular assignment, someone else will be chosen to lead. In fact, it may be preferable to move the leadership position around. For example, at many universities, a department chair serves for five years, and then steps aside for someone else to take charge.

In this atmosphere, there is no need to leave the institution when stepping down from the leadership position. The individual is seen as a valuable and respected team member. Moreover, the organization does not risk losing the wisdom of years of experience that person has to offer. So many organizations jumped on the outsourcing/downsizing bandwagon and now face the consequences of repeated mistakes, inconsistent results, and lost profits.

To build the kind of internal culture necessary for success today, it is vital to find not only teambuilders, but also individuals dedicated to uncompromising standards of quality (the shared vision).

The Need to Achieve

Why are we driven to achieve? Because it serves five basic needs of the human psyche:

- Recognition
- Economic security
- Emotional security
- Self-expression
- Self-respect

A culture of success helps people fulfill each of these needs. A culture of internal competition does not.

Again and again we must hammer this message home: *You cannot compete externally if you compete internally.*

When team members vie with each other, all players lose; when they cooperate, all players win. The key to success—on the football field and in the game of life—is that working together is the only way everyone wins.

Case Study: Home Field Advantage

Why do home team players have the advantage in an athletic struggle? Because the crowd is behind them—especially when they are winning. Hometown support builds morale and spurs players to achieve higher levels of performance.

In business, that same "home field advantage" can create a substantial psychological edge. The corporate office that cheers on and supports rather than hampers the field office's efforts to compete externally provides a much needed "home field advantage." The production department that works overtime to produce a quality custom part for a retail shop's customer is also giving the organization a "home field advantage." Once departments, divisions, and subsidiaries realize that they are all on the same team, the home field advantage can make a winner out of your organization.

Winning Strategies

The foundation of a successful culture is the deliberate initiation of win-win, cooperative strategies. Attempting to change years of reinforced competitive behavior requires a careful long-term reconditioning process.

In many enterprises, the mere thought of altering the culture is overwhelming. However, change does not have to occur all at once, or even throughout the entire organization initially. It can begin with a group that is chosen specifically to study, modify, and implement change in the system.

The one-group-at-a-time approach allows for a "mini" culture of success, where the organization, while implementing change in a particular area of responsibility, can move from a functional (vertical) to a cross-functional (horizontal) team approach in which cooperation is expected. The vertical units, often called "silos," are dismantled.

In many workplaces, individuals will need to go through a "re-learning" process during which they discover what has produced the competitive behavior and why it must be replaced with a new system based on cooperation. The entire organization must buy into the process in an intelligent, forthright manner—no tricks, no "brainwashing," and no hidden agendas.

To gain acceptance of a "shared vision" culture, leaders will need to train, train, and train some more and never stop training.

At every step, the training must apply theories from the real world of a company's product or service, and incorporate a methodical redesign of reward and recognition that reinforces cooperation.

Planning, instruction, and implementation are all vital, yet when it comes to the leader, mere words won't suffice. He or she must demonstrate what the new order really is.

As parents, we have all learned the hard way that our children listen to what we say but mimic what we do. Rather than burden the workforce with a verbal barrage of the program you envision, walk the talk day after day—with conviction—and listen carefully to those who are part of the team.

Just as conflict can produce ulcers, internal competition attacks an organization at its very heart. An enterprise cannot remain strong when it is constantly being torn apart from the inside, regardless of its history or reputation.

Vow to wage a mighty battle to defeat and eliminate the enemy within—internal competition.

Key Concepts

1. From our education systems to our workplaces, we've been conditioned to compete all our lives.

2. Internally competitive cultures undermine organizations of all sizes.

3. Autocratic leadership stimulates internal competition and divisiveness, which leads to a poor quality of goods and services, and low morale.

4. Autocratic environments work (and workers will rally) when an urgent situation demands an immediate response.

5. Democratic leadership is based on cooperation and team-oriented win-win strategies where people are respected.

6. The human psyche needs recognition, economic and emotional security, self-expression, and self-respect. A culture of success meets these needs.

7. In a totally cooperative organization, being at the top is a shared experience.

8. In a culture of success, team members ensure the leader will not fail.

9. Culture change can begin with a test group.

10. Eliminating the enemy within (internal competition) requires a long-term reconditioning process.

Things To Do Now

1. Hammer home the message that you cannot compete externally if you compete internally.

2. Find not just team builders, but individuals dedicated to uncompromising standards of quality.

3. Help individuals go through an "unlearning" process, where they learn what has produced the competitive behavior.

4. Train personnel at all levels on cooperative team skills.

5. Look for and publish success stories where an area of internal competition has been converted to internal cooperation.

6. Redesign reward and recognition systems to reinforce cooperation.

7. Ensure that leaders walk the talk.

8. Study and share models of organizations and companies who succeed with cooperative team processes.

9. Re-address the "shared vision" periodically to insure that everyone still agrees on this key focus.

8 THE ZONE OF IMPROVEMENT

We all need coaches, mentors and competitors to improve. Without teachers and challenges, we run the risk of settling for "good enough." During a televised PGA golf tournament awards ceremony, the sportscaster asked the champion, "What was the biggest factor in your victory?" The golfer replied:

> I am happy to have won, but I need to give credit for this win to Jack Nicklaus. During the practice rounds prior to the tournament, I was having great difficulty controlling my drives from the tee and I considered withdrawing from the event. When I told Jack what I was about to do, he suggested that we both go to the practice tee, to see if he could detect what I was doing wrong. There, he was able to observe and correct my problem.

The astonished announcer quickly found Jack Nicklaus. "Why would you deliberately help a competitor?" he asked the golf legend. Nicklaus replied:

> If I am unwilling to help my rivals improve, there would be no motivation for me or any other golfer to become better. Competitive golf would cease to improve.

Nicklaus understood the great principle of "raising the bar." By assisting an opponent, he increased the difficulty of the game and lifted the performance of all professional golfers. He knew all about the "zone of improvement."

The Bell Curve

Graphs can help us analyze concepts and measure success. For example, bell-shaped curves used in population studies allow us to view the normal distribution of a data sample. We can apply that metric to employee workgroups to better understand culture dynamics at work.

Figure 8.1 shows a bell-shaped curve that illustrates the performance of a typical employee workgroup.

In most groups of people, there will be high, medium and low performers. The performance of any group of people (at work, at school, or in a volunteer organization) will be distributed around the average of the entire group. The majority of the population will fall on or near the mean (average) value or score.

In Figure 8.1, we can see that 15% of employees perform below expectations and 70% perform as expected (does "expected" work and no more). That leaves a mere 15% performing above expectations.

Figure 8.1
Group Performance Expected

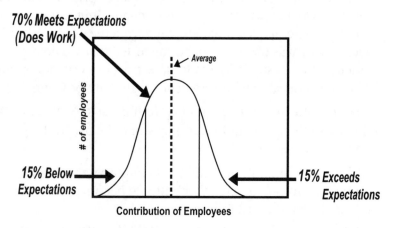

Raising the Bar

Since habit and past-learned achievement prohibits change, unless some form of intervention occurs, the results will always be the same.

The bell curve, however, is not static. It is dynamic, and its shape can be changed and repositioned. For example, if a task or learning effort is easy or routine, the bell curve will be a reflection of a wide variation in people performance.

On the other hand, if the task is demanding and everyone feels accountable for the improvement of each other, the curve will narrow and shift to the right, indicating improved performance for everyone (see Figure 8.2).

> It is only when we develop others that we permanently succeed.
> —Harvey Firestone, Industrialist

If, like Jack Nicklaus, those within an environment cooperate to help each other develop skills and learning abilities (and are accountable for the improvement of everyone), then the variability narrows and performance rises.

Notice the difference between the first bell curve and the second bell curve. The second bell curve shows a reduction in variability (curve narrows) and an increase in overall performance We call this difference the "zone of improvement." You can reach that goal by applying the culture of success principles covered in this book.

Figure 8.2
Zone of Improvement

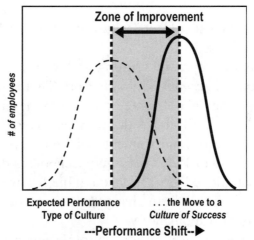

Dramatic Results

In the early 1990s, the Pinellas County School system in St. Petersburg, Florida received national acclaim by changing its educational system to include culture of success principles in its management and teaching practices. Not only did overall student performance increase, but because nearly all students were becoming better learners, the courses became more advanced to accommodate the improved performance.

Figure 8.3 shows the results of the Pinellas County School system's culture improvement efforts. Note that the dotted line that represents a traditional culture follows the bell-shaped curve of "lower expectations."

In a traditional school system, grades range from "F" to "A." In an environment of cooperation, however, where mutual accountability is practiced, the spread narrows and grades range from "C" to "A." Failure is not an option.

Instead of:
   "pick the best and forget the rest"

Enter the zone of improvement where,
   "the best perform better with the rest!"

Although the grades improved for all Pinellas County schools, the grades at the Carwise Middle School experienced success so dramatic that most students achieved A's even when tougher tests were administered.

Here is the key point: getting an "A" in a cooperative atmosphere requires *greater* skill and effort. That is what happened at Carwise Middle School, where both the highest and marginal students achieved well above the previous averages. The students entered a "zone of improvement" where everyone excelled.

The success of Pinellas County Schools is directly related to the fact that all students are accountable for everyone else's success. The *system* has been changed from one of no accountability to one of total responsibility.

In business, education, or any other endeavor, an unwillingness to contribute to each other's success ultimately erodes both quality and productivity. The result, as we have seen in education and elsewhere, is leaders being forced to "lower the bar" and accept mediocrity.

The practice of non-cooperation is harmful to the performance of all, including skilled workers and gifted students.

Figure 8.3

Grade Comparisons—Pinellas County, Florida Schools

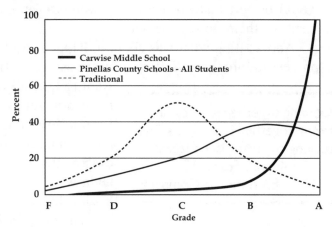

The "Leftovers"

During a three-day retreat for leaders of a 50,000-member credit union of a major corporation, we were explaining the zone of improvement, emphasizing that everyone can be an achiever if the culture is improved.

A senior manager named Andy asked if he could comment on the concept that "everyone can achieve." Andy explained that during his high school days in Columbia, Missouri, he had been a star athlete, lettering in football, basketball, and baseball each of his four years. As a freshman, he'd been asked to help organize, select, and coach intramural teams in those same sports. Andy reminded us of the all-too-familiar process of selection:

> When people really feel part of a team, managers become coaches, team members self-manage, cooperate, and help each other "raise the bar."

"All of the prospective intramural athletes met in the gym to form a pool of talent from which the star athletes would choose their teams," he explained. "Six different teams were to be formed and lots were drawn as to who would pick first, second, and so forth."

As expected, the prospects were chosen in order of their athletic ability. As the process continued, it became apparent that a few would be left that no one really wanted—an embarrassing moment for them, to say the least.

Anticipating what was about to happen, Andy interrupted the process before these "leftovers" were assigned. He announced, "I want to take all the students who have not yet been chosen, and form a seventh team." Though he knew that transforming the mediocre athletes into a competitive team would be a Herculean task, he developed a conditioning program that required everyone to run ten laps the first day of practice. They ran twenty. He asked them to do ten push-ups. They did twenty. Andy continued, "I couldn't believe it! They became self-motivated and were managing their own conditioning program."

> "Coming together is a beginning, staying together is progress, and working together is a success."
> ~Henry Ford,
> Ford Motor Company

These students honed their athletic skills faster than anyone dreamed possible. "They would have done anything for me," he stated. "All they wanted was a chance to prove themselves. All they needed was for someone to have confidence in them—someone who believed they could achieve."

With a great deal of pride in his voice, Andy noted, "During my four years at that school, the team no one wanted either tied or won the intramural championship twelve times."

Now *that* is a zone of improvement.

Remember, when people feel part of a team, managers become coaches—and often are able to shift some of their focus to other agendas.

Case Study: Harley's New Ride

During the initial production of Honda Motorcycles, Honda of America invited Harley-Davidson Motorcycle Company to visit their plant in Marysville, Ohio to study Honda's successful and profitable motorcycle operation. At the time, Harley was experiencing serious quality and productivity problems that would eventually have put them out of business. They had long been "the only domestic motorcycle manufacturer in the United States," and for years had been exhibiting the typical "don't have to change" attitude concerning management and manufacturing.

"The trouble was," says Harley-Davidson CEO Richard Teerlink, "we weren't competing against U.S. manufacturers; we were competing against the Japanese, and their methods were light-years ahead of ours."[1]

The visit to Marysville showed Harley executives in very stark terms that the vast gap in competitiveness between them and their Japanese rivals entailed different *management* approaches.

After the visit to Honda, Harley-Davidson totally embraced the creation of a success culture, and restructured its entire people management processes and manufacturing system. Today, Harley continues to be a world-class manufacturer and global player in the production of motorcycles.

Why did Honda share its knowledge with a competitor? To ensure its own continuous improvement. Honda knows that high-performance competition forces new heights of quality, intensifies team processes, escalates employee involvement, and expands quality teams to meet the new competition they have created.

The Benchmark

A leader's primary objective should be to use culture of success skills to improve the environment for all participants, not just a chosen few. Far too many leaders brag about the success of high achievers and ignore the rest.

At a recent company banquet we attended, top salespeople were presented awards. We overheard someone whisper, "The same people win year after year."

This usually happens because there is no reason for high achievers to help those who do not win.

Later, after consulting with the national sales manager, the awards were renamed "Benchmark Performers" and the criteria for winning the award included the requirement that sales leaders actively assist others to improve their performance. Their success depends on the improvement of others, often referred to as a "win-win" situation.

As Jack Nicklaus taught us, helping others to improve their performance raises the bar, which helps you improve your own performance. This process is at the heart of building a culture of success.

They Don't "Have To"

Why don't people and companies change? They don't have to. Why don't schools and students improve? They don't have to.

It was offshore competition that finally jolted American business into a "have to" mentality. And it is ironic that we have discovered that internal teamwork—people accountable to help each other improve—has created an external competitive posture that again makes us able to compete worldwide.

The trauma of 9/11 instantly created the political necessity to give attention, leadership, and significant funding to "homeland" security strategies. All future American policies and decisions will be influenced and colored by this new "have to" attitude toward domestic security. This in turn impacts attitudes at work in personal lives as well as in organizations.

> Mutual accountability lies at the foundation of any successful change for the better.

The 1980s and 1990s turn-around of American business and industry to world-class performance offers a remarkable example of a massive "zone of improvement" and is one of the great success stories in recorded history. The same "have to" attitude spurs people to seriously consider the type of culture necessary to achieve a competitive presence. Without this attitude, few organizations would risk any attempt to create a culture of success.

As noted in a 2003 statistic, 85% of American businesses, organizations, and educational institutions still do not feel the "have to" pressure to implement a contemporary, team-oriented culture of success. The methodology is available. All we need is more "take charge" and "have to do it" leadership attitudes to benefit from this knowledge.

Remember, when you help others improve, your level of achievement also soars.

We encourage businesses, schools, non-profits, and parents to use these methods to create their own "zone of improvement."

Key Concepts

1. Helping rivals improve motivates you to achieve more—it raises the bar.

2. A bell-shaped curve of a typical workgroup shows that 85% perform mediocre (average) or below-expectation work.

3. In a culture of success, where workers are focused and held accountable to help each other improve, the performance curve narrows and shifts to the right. That shift is called the "zone of improvement."

4. A system that moves from one of no accountability to one of total shared responsibility becomes a culture of success.

5. Improve the system or environment, and everyone can be an achiever!

6. The 1980s and 1990s turnaround of American business and industry to world-class performance offers a remarkable example of a massive "zone of improvement" and is one of the great success stories in business history.

7. 85% of American businesses, organizations, and educational institutions still do not feel the "have to" pressure to implement a contemporary, team-oriented culture of success.

8. Helping your external competitors brings new heights of quality, intensifies team processes, escalates employee involvement, and expands quality teams to meet the new "higher level" external competition they have created.

Things To Do Now

1. Help managers become coaches—something easy to achieve when people feel part of a team.

2. Use culture of success skills to create improvement for all participants, not just a chosen few.

3. Have your best salespeople coach your new sales trainees.

4. Develop a sense of urgency to perform better than your competition.

5. Continue to set new and higher performance goals.

6. Don't let your successes blind your need for continuous improvement. Always establish and benchmark your next set of goals.

7. Measure performance (benchmark) against global competition. This is becoming the true competition for many organizations.

8. Look for partnering opportunities with vendors, customers, and sometimes even competitors.

9. Develop a reward system that is consistent with a culture of success.

9 SIX STEPS TO SUCCESS

So far, we have been discussing the merits, methods, and mandate for establishing a culture of success. You may feel a bit overwhelmed at this point and not know where to start. Like the manager of a textile plant in South Carolina who once told us, "I know I need to transform this workforce, but where do I begin?" This chapter provides you with six steps to begin creating a culture of success in your organization.

But, before you begin using the six-step guide, consider these important points:

- Start at the top. You must ensure that the leadership is dedicated to the task and understands that a shared vision of the future means all stakeholders must be involved.

- Don't ignore the recent past. In determining the future, it is essential to examine yesterday. As Dr. Scott Sink put it in his book, *By What Method?*:

    Documenting and understanding the past and present helps avoid the impulse to promulgate the 'quick fix,' ensures continuity, helps avoid redundancy, and maximizes synergy.[1]

- Review the previous five years' performance regarding financial statistics, major personnel changes, and relationships with customers and suppliers. This information must be shared by all employees so that "everyone is on the same page" before introducing a new culture into the organization.

- Once top management is totally committed, that's the point for the transformation to begin!

People only embrace change when they:
>   Hurt enough that they are willing to change.
>   Learn enough that they want to change.
>   Receive enough that they are able to change.
>   —John C. Maxwell

The Six-Step Guide

Here is our practical six-step guide to getting started. You can use this guide to develop an agenda and determine the strategies needed for change to occur.

Step 1: Create the Team(s)

Select, at random, representatives from all levels of the organization. Group the selected candidates into teams of four to eight people, being careful to retain cross-functional representation. In small companies, the team may constitute the entire workforce. That's okay. The size of the group is not as important as the potential for creating enthusiasm and interactive behavior.

Step 2: List the Barriers

At the initial meeting of the teams, have everyone discuss the purpose and scope of the assignment. Be sure that each participant is clear on the agenda and mission. Define how "empowered" the teams are and how their recommendations to the management team will be handled.

The first task for the teams (as a group) is to use a brainstorming process to develop a list of significant "barriers" that are hindering the organization from cultivating a sense of ownership and empowerment within the organization. Figure 9.1 provides a sample list written by one such group.

Step 3: Sort Barriers Into Categories and Prepare a "Fishbone" Cause and Effect Diagram

Next, you need to select a creative process or tool to help the teams brainstorm and define key issues needing attention. We have found that the "cause and effect diagram"—commonly referred

Figure 9.1
Step 2 Sample Barriers List

Barriers to a Culture of Success	
• Closed-door policy	• No vision
• Do it my way	• Impersonal treatment
• Isolation of management	• The "big picture" is vague
• Lack of recognition	• Poor communication
• Ignoring suggestions	• Not listening
• Lack of involvement	• Fear of criticism
• Autocratic management styles	• "Perceived" inequities by employees
• Unilateral decisions	• Management indecisiveness

to as the "fishbone" or the Ishikawa diagram—does a superb job of helping teams to identify problems and their possible causes. The "fishbone" cause and effect diagram was developed by Kaoru Ishikawa during his tenure at the Kawasaki shipyards in Japan and is well known worldwide.

From the barriers list determine a category focus for each barrier. Place the category name at the end of the fishbone as shown in Figure 9.2 and list the barriers along the fishbone leading to that category. Some common categories include:

- People
- Methods
- Materials
- Equipment

You may use any category name that seems appropriate to capture and group the barriers. For our example in Figure 9.2, we selected the following categories from "The Management System" circle of the Edosomwan Model in Chapter 1 (Figure 1.1):

- Leadership
- Procedures
- Policies
- Mission & Vision
- Values
- Systems & Services

Notice in Figure 9.2 that the head of the fish is the objective (barriers to creating a culture of success) and that the bone structure shows the categories that are preventing it from happening (such as leadership, policies, and procedures). On each "bone" leading to the category is listed the barriers for that category from Step 2.

Creating a Fishbone diagram is a subjective process and group discussion is important to maintain a degree of accuracy in placing the "barrier" issues into the appropriate category.

Once your cause and effect fishbone diagram is completed, you are ready to analyze the results.

For instance, in Figure 9.2 you can see that the "impersonal treatment" barrier is one of the causes listed in the "Leadership" category. The fishbone diagram helps you identify the causes that need to be adjusted.

> The fishbone diagram is a brainstorming tool that helps a group identify the cause and effect of key barriers to creating a culture of success.

Obstacles that the teams want to take action on can then be shown in a cause-effect diagram. From these two charts, team assignments can be made to initiate corrective action. This will likely facilitate a consensus on basic root causes; an important milestone along the road to creating a culture of success.

Step 4: Quantify Barrier Data and Analyze Results

With a better grasp of the key barriers to forming a culture of success, and of the major categories for those barriers, teams must use decision-making tools to quantify the data and help them analyze the results.

As with brainstorming tools, there are many decision-making tools and processes from which to choose. We will explain two frequently used tools in this section: the "Pareto" analysis and the "Five Whys" which work hand-in-hand with the Fishbone diagram tool we used in Step 3.

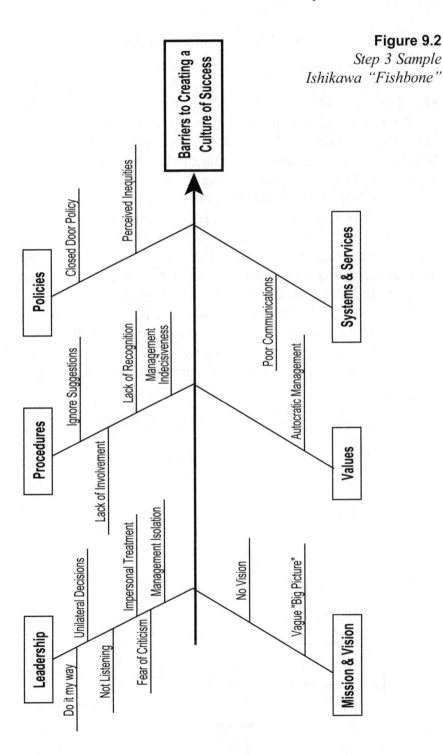

Figure 9.2
*Step 3 Sample
Ishikawa "Fishbone"*

Suggested Tool: Pareto Analysis

To add clarity and focus to the collected and applied information, a Pareto analysis (descending bar graph) can be employed to provide graphic emphasis to the category areas needing priority attention. The "Pareto" display is an excellent method to highlight what needs to be done and in what sequence. The "pareto principle" is based on the theory that careful and thorough identification of 20% of the problem sources will expose those issues that create 80% of any problem (the 80/20 rule).

To create a Pareto analysis, tabulate the frequency (number of occurrences) of barriers by category. Then, create a bar chart of the master list data. Figure 9.3 shows a sample Pareto bar chart for an organization's management system. Notice that bars of data are listed in order from left to right, from high to low.

In Figure 9.3, Leadership is the highest bar, which indicates that it is the category area needing priority attention. Investigation and improvement strategies of the barriers listed in the Fishbone diagram for this category would be appropriate focus.

Figure 9.3

Step 4 Sample Pareto Analysis for a Management System

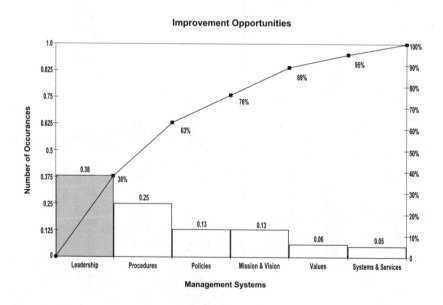

Teams should meet and display the Fishbone and Pareto diagrams side-by-side. The teams can then, individually, select one of the barriers in the highest bar category and work to determine the root cause of that barrier. The root cause is the issue(s) or condition(s) that actually created the problem in the first place.

For example, in Figure 9.2 the Fishbone diagram shows six barriers under the "Leadership" category. The team might choose "Management Isolation" as the first barrier to investigate. Once the root cause of that barrier is determined, the team selects another barrier in that highest bar category to investigate. And so on, until all of the barriers for that category have been addressed.

> The Pareto Analysis bar graph is a discussion tool that helps people focus their energies on the highest priority barriers to creating a culture of success.

This process is repeated. As soon as all the barriers in the highest bar category are treated and corrected, a revised Pareto chart is prepared. The revised Pareto analysis provides a graphic display of culture changes made and clearly shows the next area on which to focus. If your culture changes were successful, a different category will emerge in the highest bar position and the process is repeated on the barriers in that category.

Suggested Tool: The Five Whys Technique

How are you going to find out the root cause of a barrier? Again, there are many decision-modeling processes and tools from which to choose. We've found most people respond well to a "drill down" method named the "Five Whys" technique. Developed by a Toyota engineer, Taiichi Ohno, this simple process, when applied to a problem, can be an excellent method of finding the root cause of a problem.

The Five Whys technique is a brainstorming method intended to be used in a team environment. Basically, the root cause of a problem is determined by asking *why* a problem exists. The answer is then rephrased as another why question. By repeatedly asking the question "why?" of the answers given you can usually drill-down to the root cause of a problem.

Here are the steps involved:

- Identify the barrier to be analyzed.
- Ask *Why?* this barrier exists.
- Each time the question is answered, ask *Why?* again.
- Continue to ask *Why?* until everyone involved is satisfied they have arrived at the root cause of that barrier.

Using the Fishbone diagram in Figure 9.2, here is an example of a Five Whys analysis for the Leadership barrier, "Impersonal Treatment:"

1. Why are managers impersonal with workers?

  ‣ Because we have always done it that way.

2. Why have we always done it that way?

  ‣ Because we know of no other way.

3. Why do we not know any other way?

  ‣ Because we have not had appropriate training to learn participative and cooperative styles of leadership and management. And, we do not see our management walking the talk, listening to others, or inviting their involvement.

4. Why have we not had appropriate leadership and management training?

  ‣ Because we have never had to!

In this example, using only four whys, we have discovered the root cause of management isolation—*there is no pressure or reason to do so*. It is not necessary to use all of the five whys. The process is designed to use the "why" question until you identify the root cause (could be greater or fewer than five whys).

Selecting Decision Modeling Tools

While we have only used three decision-modeling tools (Fishbone, Pareto, and Five Whys) in this chapter, it is important to note that many other tools are available to assist you in making better decisions. The value of decision-making tools is two-fold:

- Easier and more accurate decision-making.
- Graphic display of the data being considered.

Most people understand an issue better when it is displayed in a graphic format. Further examples, explanations, and in-depth instructions on how to use and select decision making tools can be found on the Internet or in such books as *The Memory Jogger* and *The Quality Toolbox*.[2]

Step 5: Publish the Results and Create the Agenda for Change

The next step is to publish the task force team results so that every employee can see the issues that challenge the future of the organization. The items to be addressed (root cause of barriers) become the *agenda for change* that will be assigned to the various groups.

Step 6: Form Action Teams and Move Toward Continuous Improvement

Form "action teams" to start developing the new processes and systems that will pave the way for change. These may be the same ones, or new. Free group members so that each can spend a concentrated amount of time on this important task.

Each team should develop a specific objective. Once again, top management must communicate the scope of the work and define the team's empowerment.

Recommendations from working groups will be discussed at the highest levels of the company. What is management going to do with them? This needs serious discussion before moving on to the next item.

The newly designed systems and resulting processes will likely require organizational structure changes to accommodate the new atmosphere of cooperation. People are now moving out of their "turf" mentality and beginning to work in a multi-functional environment for the success of the entire organization.

Now coordinate the efforts of the various teams into a unified strategy that can be shared with all employees.

It is here that the concept of *continuous improvement should be introduced*—if it has not been already. An open forum is needed for ongoing recommendations and suggestions from an entire workforce now both involved and committed.

Remember, you are making progress as a group, not as individuals.

It Works!

What happens to workers when management asks them to become part of the decision-making team? They become invested, your success becomes their success.

It won't happen by snapping your fingers. You can't keep people on your payroll for twenty years without asking their opinions, and then expect them to become a fountain of ideas instantly. In time, however, they will change. It takes two to six years.

When a Ford plant in Cincinnati moved to a system of total worker involvement, only twenty-five of the 2,500 employees couldn't make the transition. What does that tell us? 99% of employees are capable of making the change from a controlled, autocratic environment into an entrepreneurial, democratic workplace.

What happens when culture of success principles are activated? Workers thrive and quality skyrockets!

Culture Impacts Profits

Still not convinced? Need further proof? The Denison Organizational Culture Survey was designed to measure the influence of performance culture on the bottom line.

This highly reputable study of 161 publicly traded companies provides direct evidence of the cause and effect relationship between work culture and profits.

As you can see in Appendix A, the Denison Organizational Culture Survey diagram shows a much higher Return on

Stockholder's Equity (ROE=21%) for high performance cultures than for low performance cultures (ROE=6%). They also report very similar results for Return on Total Investment.

Are You Ready?

Have you made the commitment to see your organization emerge as a culture of success example?

If so, realize that what we've been addressing is much more than another "program of the month." It is a permanent way of life that will forever transform you and the rest of your organization.

Never stop asking the vital questions:

☑ Is every stakeholder involved?

☑ Is the vision of the future a shared dream?

☑ Does the vision address *culture*?

☑ Has the mission statement become an agenda everyone will support?

☑ Has the impact of the changes been taken into account?

☑ Am I committed to uncompromising quality at every level of product and service?

☑ Do I have the courage to "stay the course" regardless of the barriers we will encounter?

☑ Does the reward system support the behaviors we want?

If your answer is an unqualified "yes," you are ready for the most exciting journey of your life.

Welcome to the *culture of success!*

Key Concepts

1. Before you can use the six-step guide to building a culture of success, leadership must be dedicated to the task. Also, a study of the recent history should be performed including the past five years performance.

2. Create teams from all levels of the organization.

3. Teams should list barriers they see to creating a culture of success.

4. Teams must be empowered and told how their recommendations to management will be handled.

5. Use group discussion tools to help analyze the barrier lists.

6. An Ishikawa "Fishbone" diagram can be used to organize the barriers list by categories.

7. The frequency of barriers across teams can be computed and organized into a Pareto chart (a bar chart in descending order by frequency).

8. The Pareto analysis is also known as the 80/20 rule: identifying 20% of the problem sources exposes the issues that create 80% of any problem.

9. Using the Pareto chart, various decision-modeling tools can be used to investigate the root cause of each barrier in the primary bar.

10. The "Five Whys" is a group discussion tool which helps identify the root cause of a given problem.

11. The data and analysis should be published and shared with all employees. The items to be addressed become the agenda for change.

12. Action teams are formed to carry out the agenda for change.

13. As newly-designed systems and resulting processes are introduced, the concept of continuous improvement must be explained.

14. It takes two to six years for an organization to convert from a controlled, autocratic environment to an entrepreneurial, democratic workplace.

15. A culture of success is not a flavor of the month strategy, but a permanent way of life that will forever transform you and your organization.

Things To Do Now

Follow the six steps outlined in this chapter, referring back to the prior chapters in this book and appendices as needed to garner support and understanding for moving toward a culture of success.

APPENDICES

APPENDIX A: QUICK COURSE ON QUALITY

The word "quality" can apply to the culture in which we function, as well as to conventional products and services. In fact, some of the principles that produce excellent quality in products and services can be used to produce a "quality" culture. This appendix provides you with a brief background on service/product-based "quality" initiatives (generally referred to as "Total Quality Management" or TQM) and explains which aspects can be used in creating a culture of success.

Measuring Performance

In the early 1980s, consumers began to demand *quality*. Today, *quality* is a given. In less than two decades, we've moved as consumers from accepting inferior products and services, to demanding better quality, to assuming we'll get high quality products and services for our dollar.

That's a lot of change in a short period of time, but the roots of such change stem back farther. Before the days of mass production, each segment of a product was handcrafted and fitted together individually. Then things changed radically. As mass-produced components and interchangeable parts became available, and tolerances and standard dimensions insured that they would fit together perfectly, conformity rose to top priority, and statistical quality measurement became a vital industrial tool.

On thousands of assembly lines, companies measured workers' performance. Scientific management theories, and resulting "division of labor" techniques, developed that broke tasks into subcomponents. Workers became proficient—and often bored— at these repetitive tasks.

Today, managers consider productivity, performance, and variation to be essential management tools. But not everyone agrees on the definition of excellence, which is why the focus of this book is devoted to cooperative working environments, which tend to shrink variation while increasing performance and quality. But before you can implement a cooperative working environment, you need to understand the quality theories that have come before and what aspects of those theories you can use to build a culture of success.

Statistical Quality Control

World War II spawned a new enthusiasm for statistical quality control. Almost overnight, industrial companies began using statistical quality control to produce higher quality products at a lower cost per unit. This movement was documented by Eugene L. Grant, professor of economics and engineering at Stanford University:

> The spectacular savings in man power and materials that resulted from certain wartime applications of statistical quality control have often generated much enthusiasm... In hundreds of industrial companies that had made little or no use of these techniques, their use is now accepted as routine and commonplace cost-savings matter. [1]

Many decades later, management is beginning to realize that gathering statistics and applying them in a narrow way, department by department, function by function, in a plethora of disorganized and uncoordinated efforts is not producing the quality or cost savings they had hoped.

Gathering statistics is all well and good, but what applications of these new facts promise to help make an organization or manufacturing plant more effective? A better approach is what we call the "Total Approach:"

1. Tailor-make each application for the specific circumstance. To do this, form a group of employees who can combine their knowledge of statistical principles with an understanding of design, production, sales, and budgeting.

2. Realize that nearly all applications cross the lines of departmental authority. For any effort to yield quality results, the team must include the leaders of each department in the planning, implementation, and analysis phases of the application.

Quality: The Human Dimension

Ironically, the study of statistical quality control, measuring the variation in processes and machines, led to the TQM movement which embraced the performance of individual workers.

Organizations began to realize that after implementing advances in science and technology, for all new efficiencies gained, inevitably, they had to face an unfortunate by-product: an impersonal approach. Why is that important? Because when all is said and done, organizations remain, essentially, human organizations.[2]

No one is arguing that scientific and technical advances haven't provided us with new knowledge and business tools. But these are only part of the puzzle. Another portion, one almost forgotten during that period of fixation on efficiency, is that humans still control organizations, and therefore, the new efficiencies remain driven by an unpredictability of human initiatives and responses.

> You can accomplish anything in life, provided you don't mind who gets the credit.
>
> **—Harry S. Truman**

The challenge we face is to reverse the depersonalization of business and industry that dates back to the industrial revolution and the English factory system.

Can statistical profiles help in the selection process of a new employee? Yes. Can highly-technical training programs add to the predictability of success? Yes. But, these elements are only part of what it takes to attain a culture of success.

Next, you will learn about the people who put the human element back into the equation: Deming, Juran, and Crosby.

The Deming Method

A recipient of the National Medal of Technology from President Reagan in 1987, Dr. W. Edwards Deming is revered as a pioneer of statistical quality control.

While completing his Ph.D. in physics at Yale in the 1920s, Deming spent his summers working at companies like Western Electric's Hawthorne plant in Chicago. There, while observing workers who were paid by the piece and who suffered docked pay if a piece failed inspection, Deming came to the conclusion that "Piecework is man's lowest degradation."[3]

A few years later, in 1927, Deming was working at the U.S. Department of Agriculture and met Dr. Walter A. Shewhart, a physicist, who was conducting statistical studies at Bell Telephone Laboratories. Dr. Shewhart developed a method called "statistical control" that set the acceptable highs and lows for product quality. The beauty of Shewhart's method was that he trained the employee to do the charting—giving employees greater control over their jobs and allowing them to make adjustments on their own. To Deming, Shewhart's genius was in recognizing when to act and when to leave a process alone.

Total Quality Management reminds us:

- Attitudes and emotions remain the primary influences on an organization.
- Values, aspirations, and beliefs saturate the substance of knowledge and reason.
- The laws and principles of physical science should not be used to predict human behavior.
- The larger the enterprise, the more it takes on a personality and momentum of its own.
- People change their minds or habits, and no mathematical formula can predict that change.
- People come to work each day with their own agenda.

Inspired by Shewhart, Deming tried to promote his ideas to business and industry. Not long after the end of World War II, feeling rebuffed that some of his theories were not being accepted by U.S. businesses, Deming began to spend a great deal of time in Japan. His work there was widely accepted and today Deming is heralded as the person who is largely responsible for making Japan's high-quality production the envy of the world.

Deming believed that the only way for a product to become superior was to allow the people doing the work to conduct their own self-inspection. Quality, he taught, stems primarily from human commitment.

Deming developed a comprehensive management strategy based on this philosophy:

A company must never stop improving the quality of its products or services, and must have the singular goal of satisfying its customers.

This philosophy could be viewed as the "shared vision" or common goal that binds the workers and management at all levels. Deming taught that to be successful, an organization must embrace and implement this philosophy at every level—in effect, transforming the company's entire culture. The change must begin with, and be led by, top management.

Again, we have the lesson that the management system has the most power, and thus must lead the change, drive the culture.

Deming believed that management needed to stop focusing on dividend and stock value increases. Instead, he urged management to serve stockholders better by staying in business with constant improvements to product quality, which in turn leads to decreased costs, market expansion, new jobs, and greater profits.

Quality Management is all about customer focus, continual improvement, and making sure quality is factored into each of your processes and products... Without quality management, it is difficult to identify if a real system is in place or if it is just a few dynamic individuals holding things together.[4]

Summary of Deming's Method[5]:

1. Adopt the philosophy of continuous quality improvement for every aspect of the company.

2. Build quality into work processes and the employee mindset.

3. Work with suppliers to develop long-term quality relationships rather than awarding business merely on the basis of price.

4. Take fear out of the workplace and provide workers with the training required to ensure that they have the information and resources to do the job right.

5. Educate workers about quality improvement, eliminate numerical quotas, and remove barriers to pride of workmanship.

6. Break down the walls between different groups within the organization.

7. Develop and carry out a plan of action to accomplish all of the above.

Deming taught that quality was primarily a function of human commitment. His "human" approach to implementing statistical controls opened the door for others such as Juran and Crosby.

The Juran Method

Whereas Deming focused mainly on the application of statistical controls to identify variation, Dr. Joseph M. Juran addressed methods for managing quality control. In his early years, Juran worked as a chief inspector of the control division at Western Electric. Like Deming, Juran was greatly influenced by Walter Shewhart's statistical control theories.

Juran gained respect and prominence when his theories were embraced by postwar Japan. And, in many ways Juran's approach heavily influenced the evolution of Deming's theories from a relatively narrow focus on statistical process control techniques to a comprehensive management philosophy.[6]

Juran recognized, perhaps before anyone else, that quality can be a vehicle for significant organizational change.

Summary of Juran's Method[7]:

- Quality is a customer-oriented concept best defined as "fitness for use."
- The user is the ultimate judge of how a product will be used.
- A product's goal should include "freedom from waste, freedom from trouble, and freedom from failure."
- Employee involvement is essential in achieving quality improvement.
- Management is directly responsible for the success or failure of the system.
- Total quality requires leaders to champion an ongoing shift in corporate consciousness.
- A company will meet its quality objectives only when every department in the company participates.

Juran offered three pillars to guide us:

1. Quality planning means developing superior products and processes that meet customer needs.
2. Quality improvement means reaching new levels of performance by eliminating the causes of chronic waste in work processes.
3. The definition of quality control is to maintain optimal effectiveness by measuring performance against standards and taking necessary corrective action.

Whereas Deming taught us that quality was primarily a function of human commitment, Juran taught that the user is the final judge of quality. Like Deming, Juran reminds us that management is directly responsible for the success or failure of a system. Once again, management is seen as the most powerful force that must drive culture changes.

And lastly, Juran was perhaps the first to recognize that quality can be a vehicle for cultural change. Quality as a shared vision being one of the elements needed in creating a culture of success.

The Crosby Method

Another cornerstone in total quality management theory isby Philip B. Crosby. Crosby worked for the Martin Company in the early 1960s and brought tremendous personal energy and enthusiasm to the TQM movement. His book, *Quality Is Free*, was required reading at every executive level. In his book, he preached four "absolutes" of quality management which will we summarize here as the Crosby Method.

Summary of the Crosby Method:

1. *The definition of quality is conformance to requirements.* The customer defines the requirement and specifications are drawn. There is no room for error.

2. *The system of quality is prevention.* Quality must be in the design and work process, not a review of the final result.

3. *The performance standard of quality is zero defects.* Products or services must conform to the requirements completely. The entire organization must be committed to perfection and a nonconforming product must never be delivered under any circumstances.

4. *The measurement of quality is the price of nonconformance.* The cost of quality is the price of conformance plus the price of nonconformance. Eliminating errors through quality improvements decreases the total cost of production.

Crosby's "zero defects" approach to quality control is the forerunner to the popular Six Sigma tool, which means minimizing variation. Crosby takes a proactive approach to quality. Quality in his eyes is a system of prevention, not inspection. Likewise, a quality culture requires daily attention, not annual fixing.

Case Study: How Japan's Culture Drove USA to Quality

Why did post-war Japan rush to adopt the concepts of Deming and Juran? The key may be in the Japanese culture. According to Dr. M. R. Ramsay, United Nations labor advisor, with their "unique power of observation, sincere studiousness, and a determined effort to learn and succeed, the Japanese persevered and achieved."[8]

In 1946, Japan formed the Union of Japanese Scientists and Engineers (JUSE) to promote the advancement of science and technology. In the early 1950s JUSE invited quality experts like Deming and Juran to teach their methods, which were quickly adopted. A decade later, JUSE introduced the innovative concept of quality circles to the Japanese workplace. By the 1970s, the results were so spectacular that the U.S. began hiring Japanese consultants to train the leaders of companies like Lockheed, General Motors, and Westinghouse.

At this point, Japan was so successful that American business and industry had no choice but to embrace the quality message.

Which Method Is Best?

As you will see in this book, creating a culture of success requires that you use elements from all three methods. But, more important than the approach chosen is the company's willingness to commit to and persevere in executing that choice, until quality is achieved. Yet another "shared vision" building block.

Key Concepts

1. Scientific management, which promised higher quality at lower cost through division of labor, had an unintended by-product: it prompted an impersonal approach that alienated workers.

2. The study of statistical quality control inevitably led to the realization of the importance of the human element in any process, system, or organization.

3. TQM focused on bringing integrity and control back to the worker.

4. Dr. W. Edwards Deming, influenced by Dr. Walter A. Shewhart, embraced the concept of giving workers greater control over their jobs.

5. Deming taught that quality was primarily a function of human commitment.

6. Dr. Joseph M. Juran addressed methods for managing quality, helping turn Deming's theories into a more comprehensive philosophy.

7. Juran taught that the customer is the final judge of quality. Moreover, Juran recognized that quality can be a vehicle for cultural change within an organization.

8. Japan adopted the TQM concepts from Deming and Juran decades before the U.S. competition with Japan forced American business to finally embrace the quality message.

9. Philip B. Crosby took a proactive approach to quality control. He saw quality as a system of prevention, not inspection.

10. Crosby's zero defects approach is a forerunner to the popular Six Sigma tool used by many businesses today.

11. Various aspects of TQM can be used to create a culture of success.

Things To Do Now

1. Combine knowledge of statistics with an understanding of design, production, sales, and budgeting.

2. Help employees realize that nearly all activities now cross departmental lines.

3. Reverse the depersonalization of statistical analysis tools.

4. Never stop improving the quality of your company's products and services.

5. Make satisfying customers your primary goal.

6. Initiate and lead change.

7. Study the criteria for the ISO standards such as ISO-9000 and QS-9000 to structure a foundation for change based on the documentation of methods and processes that support quality improvement efforts. For more information, see their website: www.ISO.org.

8. Consider using the Baldridge National Quality Award criteria to establish leadership and management goals. For more information, see their website: www.quality.nist.gov.

APPENDIX B:
DENISON SURVEY

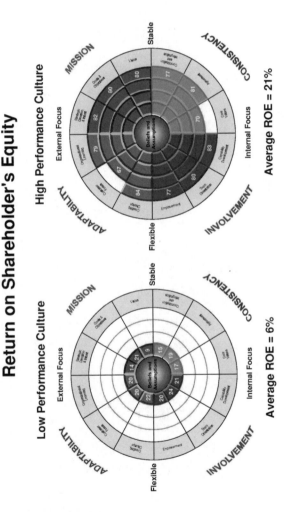

Return on Shareholder's Equity

Low Performance Culture   High Performance Culture

Average ROE = 6%   Average ROE = 21%

- Study of 161 publicly traded companies from a broad range of industries
- Contrasts the performance of the 10% of the organizations with the best culture scores with the 10% of the organization with the worst culture scores
- Average ROE for the organizations with the lowest culture scores is 6%, Average ROE for organizations with high culture scores is 21%
- Highly similar results for return on total investment

NOTES

Authors' Note

1. Charles B. Dygert and Richard A. Jacobs, *The Culture of Success*. Ohio: MEI, Inc., 1996.

Introduction

1. William Byham and Jeff Cox, *Zapp*. New York: Ballantine Books; Revised Edition, 1997.

Chapter 1

1. Gilbert Fuchsberg, "Quality Programs Show Shoddy Result," *Wall Street Journal*, May 14, 1992. p. B-1.

2. Dr. Johnson Edosomwan, *Edosomwan Organizational and Process Reengineering*, Los Angeles: Saint Lucie Press; 1995. Organizational and Process Transformation Model by Dr. Johnson A. Edosomwan, © 1994 Edosomwan and JJA Consultants, Inc. All rights reserved. Reprinted in this book by permission of Dr. Edosomwan and JJA Consultants.

3. Sun Tzu, *The Art of War* (translation by Thomas Cleary), Boston: Shambhala Publications, 1988, pp.7-8.

4. Noel Tichy and Strafford Sherman, *Control Your Own Destiny or Someone Else Will*, New York: Harper Busines Press, 1994, p. 7.

5. Christopher I. Barnard, *The Functions of the Executive*, Cambridge, MA: Harvard University Press, 1938, pp. 233-234.

Chapter 2

1. Cecil Murphey, *Simply Living: Modern Wisdom from the Ancient Book of Proverbs*, London: Westminster John Knox Press, 2001.

2. *The Advocate*, Newark, Ohio, front page headline Monday February 4, 2002, by Richard Weiner, *USA Today*.

3. Jon R. Katzenbach and Douglas K. Smith, *The Wisdom of Teams*, New York: Harper Business Press, 1993, p. 3.

4. Infinity Broadcasting, interview with Army General Tommy Franks aired Thursday, March 27, 2003.

5. Elliot Jaques, *The Changing Culture of a Factory*, London: Taylor & Francis Books Ltd. 1951 [reprinted 2003 by Routledge].

6. Elliot Jaques, *Requisite Organization: A Total System for Effective Managerial Organization and Managerial Leadership for the 21st Century: Amended,* Gloucester, Massachusetts: Cason Hall and Co. Publishers, 1998. Quoted material taken from cover jacket.

7. Ibid., p.136.

Chapter 3

1. Rundell C. Reid, "NASDC: A Businessman's Experience, Phi Delta Kappa, December, 1992. p. 290.

2. Terrence E. Deal and Allan A. Kennedy, *Corporate Cultures: The Rites and Rituals of Corporate Life*, Boulder, Colorado: Perseus Publishing, 2000, p. 22.

3. Dennis Kinlaw, *Developing Superior Work Teams*, Lexington, MA: Lexington Books, 1991, p. 26.

Chapter 4

1. Terrence E. Deal and Allan A. Kennedy, *Corporate Cultures: The Rites and Rituals of Corporate Life*, Boulder, Colorado: Perseus Publishing, 2000, p. 85.

2. Julia Boorstin, "The 100 Best Companies to Work For—J.M.Smucker is No. 1," *Fortune*, January 12, 2004.

3. Harry Levinson, "Why Behemoths Fail—Psychological Roots of Corporate Failure," *American Psychologist*, May 1994, p. 429.

4. Sir Brian Pitman, "Leading for Value," *Harvard Business Review*, April 2003, p. 46

5. Douglas McGregor, *Leadership and Motivation*, Cambridge, MA: M.I.T. Press, 1966, p. 121.

Chapter 5

1. Ken Kivenko, "Improve Performance by Driving Out Fear," *Quality Progress*, Oct. 1994, p. 77..

2. David Kearns, quoted in Snyder, Dowd and Houghton, *Vision, Values, and Courage—Leadership for Quality Management*, New York: The Free Press, 1994, p. 31.

3. William Eaton, quoted in Brian Dumaine, "The Bureaucracy Busters," *Fortune*, June 17, 1991, p. 50.

Chapter 6

1. Gregg Foster, quoted in Robert A. Mamis, "Man of Iron," *Inc.*, January, 1992, p. 58.

Chapter 7

1. Daniel Goleman, *Emotional Intelligence: Why It Can Matter More Than IQ*, New York: Bantam Books, 1995. [secondary reference] *The crash of the intimidating pilot: Carl Lavin*, "When Moods Affect Safety: Communications in a Cockpit Mean a Lot a Few Miles Up," *New York: The New York Times,* June 26, 1994.

2. Del Jones, "Autocratic Leadership Works—Until it Fails," Washington, DC: *USA Today,* June 6, 2003, p. 4A.

Chapter 8

1. Richard Teerlink, quoted in Peter C. Reid, *Well Made in America*, New York: McGraw-Hill, 1990, p.19.

Chapter 9

1. Scott Sink, "VPC's Grand Strategy System," VQPC Fall Newsletter, 1992, p. 8.

2. Michael Brassard, *The Memory Jogger Plus+: Featuring the Seven Management and Planning Tools*, Salem, NH: GOAL/QPC, 1996.

   Nancy R. Rague, *The Quality Toolbox*, American Society for QualityQuality Press, Milwaukee, WI: 1995.

Appendix A

1. Eugene L.Grant, *Statistical Quality Control* (Second edition), New York: McGraw-Hill, 1952, p. ix.

2. J. Douglas Brown, *The Human Nature of Organizations*, New York: AMACON, 1973, p. 1.

3. Neil H. Snyder, James J. Dowd, Jr. and Dianne M. Houghton, *Visions, Values and Courage — Leadership for Quality Management*, New York: The Free Press, 1994, p. 31.

4. W. Edwards Deming, quoted in Mary Walton, *The Deming Management Method*, New York: Putnam Publishing, p. xi of the foreword.

5. Snyder, Dowd and Houghton, p. 35.

6. Ibid., p. 38.

7. J. M. Juran, Quality Control Handbook, New York: McGraw-Hill,1951, p. 14.

8. Dr. M. R. Ramsay, "Quality and Productivity Toward 2000 and Beyond," QPM, *Industrial and Systems Engineering*, College of Engineering, Virginia Tech, Vol 10, Number 1, 1992, p. 18.

Appendix B

1. *Return on Shareholder's Equity* chart reprinted by permission of Denison Consulting, © 2004 Denison Consulting, all rights reserved. Dr. Daniel Denison created the Denison model which is the basis for the Organizational Culture Survey (developed with William S. Neale). For more information, please see the Denison website at www.DenisonCulture.com.

ACKNOWLEDGMENTS

No book is born without the help of others. Our journey to this second edition was no exception. First and foremost, we would like to thank our many clients and colleagues over the years who allowed us to be a part of their organizations and share our culture improvement techniques. The lessons learned from serving them are the foundation for this book, and thus, this book would never have been possible without them.

We would like to thank Neil Eskelin who took our first collection of lecture notes and distilled them into the first edition of this book. And, we would like to thank the staff at Moo Press Business Books for working with us through the numerous updates and helping us organize the revised manuscript into a solid guidebook for anyone interested in improving the culture where they work or volunteer.

Many thanks to the readers of the first edition, and most recently, to our peer group reviewers who read the draft manuscript and provided valuable feedback and constructive criticism that shaped the final book. We especially thank the following colleagues who gave graciously of their time: Ted Coons, Ray Forbes, Ph.D., Paul Greenland, Jackie Hammonds, Cris Holtzmuller, Jim Hopkins, Chuck Hossom, Ginnie McDevitt, George Smith, Ph.D., and Dan Toussant.

A special thank you goes out to Gregg Foster from Charles Dygert, not only as an early reader, but as a person who encouraged the first book's publication and motivated Charles to write *Success is A Team Effort,* and with Rich Jacobs write *Managing for Success.* Thank you, Gregg, for your early and continued support and encouragement.

Finally, we would like to thank our families for their patience and support; especially our wives Donna Dygert and Ingrid Jacobs who helped us in so many ways.

ABOUT THE
AUTHORS

Charles B. Dygert, Ph.D. began his career as a tool and die maker for General Motors. He earned his Bachelors, Masters, and Doctorate degrees from The Ohio State University and served on their faculty for nineteen years. For seven years of his university career, Dygert served as a management specialist with the Ohio Department of Development, Economic Development Team, the same Development Team that brought Honda of America to Ohio. He is a Certified Speaking Professional and was awarded the Council of Peers Award for Excellence, both designations of the National Speakers Association. As a distinguished speaker on leadership, motivation, productivity, and team building, he has given over 2,500 presentations in all fifty states and in several foreign countries during the past twenty-five years. Author of the acclaimed book, *Success is a Team Effort*, Dygert is currently serving as an Adjunct Faculty member for Franklin University's School of Business MBA program.

Richard A. Jacobs, P.E., is a former CEO who has led many business turnarounds and cultural transformations. His values developed as he worked summers as a laborer in a glass plant. His first management job was in a glass plant some fifteen years later. Brockway, Inc., a Fortune 500 packaging company until it was sold in 1987, was where Jacobs "practiced" and honed his management skills. Jacobs was president of Brockway Plastics, Inc. and later president and CEO of National Gas & Oil Corporation. Jacobs is a registered engineer in Pennsylvania and Ohio.

After nearly thirty-five years of supervising, managing, and leading others, Jacobs decided to pursue mentoring, teaching, and writing as a career. Jacobs is currently a "TEC Chair" in Columbus, Ohio where he coaches CEOs. He has taught in the MBA program at Franklin University where he works with his co-author, Charles Dygert. Jacobs earned his undergraduate degree from The Pennsylvania State University and his master's from Lehigh University.

Jacobs and his wife, Ingrid, reside on a hilltop outside Granville, Ohio high above the city lights where deer and wild turkey frequent the neighborhood.

Quick Order Form

🖨 Fax this form to: 845-987-7845

☎ Telephone: 845-987-7750
(have your credit card ready)

💻 Email orders: orders@MooPress.com
(or order online at www.MooPress.com)

✉ Postal Orders: Moo Press, Inc. PO Box 54 Warwick, NY 10990

☐ **YES**, please send me the following copies of *Creating a Culture of Success.*

QTY	PRICE	TOTAL
_____ X	$19.95 =	_____
Shipping & Handling*		_____
Sales Tax**		_____
Total Amount Due		_____

* Shipping costs: Ground — $ 4 first book, $1 each addl.
Express — $12 first book, $2 each addl.
Bulk orders: call for best shipping rates and qty. discount.
**Please add on 8.5% sales tax for books shipped to NY.

Payment

☐ Check ☐ Visa ☐ Mastercard ☐ Amex ☐ Discover
Please make checks payable to **Moo Press, Inc.**

Card Number: _____ Exp. Date: ___/___

Name (print): _____ Signature: _____

Organization: _____

Billing Address: _____

City: _____ State: _____ Zip: _____

Note: If you would like to have books shipped to a different address than your billing address, please provide that address on the back of this form or on a separate page.

Thank you for your order!

Share The Journey

Tell Us Your Story

We hope that this book has inspired you and your organization to fine-tune the heart and soul of your organization. We invite you to share your story with us as you embark on this journey to a culture of success. Tell us what obstacles you faced, what methods worked, and which concepts did not hold true for you. We will gather this information and incorporate it into the next edition. Help us "raise the bar" for future readers.

Send your culture of success story, feedback, comments, and suggestions to:

Culture of Success

Moo Press, Inc.

PO Box 54

Warwick, NY 10990

Or, write comments below and fax to 845-987-7845:

_____

_____

_____

_____

_____

_____

Thank you!

Want to share *Creating A Culture of Success* with someone?
Use the **Quick Order Form** on the back of this page.